Jeff You

C000301141

Bright Ph

With lyrics by Martin Heslop

Bloomsbury Methuen Drama

An imprint of Bloomsbury Publishing Plc

B L O O M S B U R Y

LONDON • NEW DELHI • NEW YORK • SYDNEY

Bloomsbury Methuen Drama

An imprint of Bloomsbury Publishing Plc

Imprint previously known as Methuen Drama

50 Bedford Square	1385 Broadway
London	New York
WC1B 3DP	NY 10018
UK	USA

www.bloomsbury.com

BLOOMSBURY, METHUEN DRAMA and the Diana logo
are trademarks of Bloomsbury Publishing Plc

First published 2014

Script © Jeff Young 2014
Lyrics © Martin Heslop 2014

British Library Cataloguing-in-Publication Data
A catalogue record for this book is available from the British Library

ISBN: PB: 978-1-4742-2880-0
ePDF: 978-1-4742-2881-7
ePub: 978-1-4742-2882-4

Library of Congress Cataloging-in-Publication Data
A catalog record for this book is available from the Library of Congress

Series: Modern Plays

Typeset by Country Setting, Kingsdown, Kent CT14 8ES
Printed and bound in Great Britain

Liverpool Everyman & Playhouse
present the world première of

BRIGHT PHOENIX

by Jeff Young

with lyrics by Martin Heslop

First performed on 3 Oct 2014
at the Everyman Theatre, Liverpool

LIVERPOOL EVERYMAN & PLAYHOUSE
Two Great Theatres. One Creative Heart.

We are two distinct theatres, almost a mile apart, which together make up a single artistic force.

For over ten years we have been driven by our passion for our art form, our love of our city and our unswerving belief that theatre at its best can enhance lives. While our two performance bases could hardly be more different, they are united by our commitment to brilliant, humane, forward-thinking theatre that responds to its time and place.

Our mission is to reflect the aspirations and concerns of our audiences, to dazzle and inspire them, welcome and connect with them, nurture the artists within them and fuel their civic pride. Wherever these connections happen – whether in our theatres, in the community, in schools, or outside Liverpool – we hope to ignite the imagination, explore what it is to be human and always to exceed expectation.

At the beating heart of the theatres is our work with writers, since it is our passionate belief that an investment in new writing is an investment in our theatrical future. Our mission is to nurture and develop the playwrights who will represent the city's talent, its voice and its unique energy, while at the same time showcasing new work by established local, national and international playwrights. In the last ten years we have produced 38 world premières across the two theatres, three quarters of which were by Liverpool writers. Of these, ten were debut plays and fifteen of the productions toured or transferred.

We are two buildings with many audiences and communities, brought together by a sincere belief that theatre at its best transforms lives.

For more information about the Everyman & Playhouse, including the full programme and activities such as playwright support visit www.everymanplayhouse.com

0151 709 4776
everymanplayhouse.com

Twitter.com/LivEveryPlay
Flickr.com/LivEveryPlay
Instagram.com/LivEveryplay

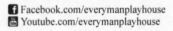

Facebook.com/everymanplayhouse
Youtube.com/everymanplayhouse

THANK YOU

We are a registered charity (1081229) and gratefully acknowledge the support of our funders, donors and audiences.

For their ongoing financial support, we would like to thank:

 Supported using public funding by **ARTS COUNCIL ENGLAND**

 Liverpool City Council

Esmée Fairbairn Foundation,
Paul Hamlyn Foundation,
The Leverhulme Trust,
Knowsley Mbc

Our Principal Partner:
Liverpool John Moores University

Our Business Members and Sponsors:

Benson Signs, Bolland & Lowe, Bruntwood,
Cobhams Tax Consultants and Accountants, DTM Legal,
Duncan Sheard Glass, EEF, Exterion Media, Home Bargains,
Hope Street Hotel, Liverpool City Region LEP, Morecrofts,
The Nadler Hotel Liverpool, PWD Solutions, Synergy,
Wrightsure Insurance Group

Those who have left us a legacy:
Dorothy Smellie
Anni Parker and Brian Barry
Malcolm and Roger Frood in memory of Graham and Joan Frood

And all the individual donors listed on our website at
www.everymanplayhouse.com

Credits

Cast

Carl Au	Alan 'Icarus' Flynn
Paul Duckworth	Lucas Firebright
Rhian Green	The entire population of Lime Street
Penny Layden	Lizzie Flynn
Rhodri Meilir	Spike Smith
Mark Rice-Oxley	Stephen Shakey
Cathy Tyson	Elsie Barmaid
Keiran Urquhart	Calumn Flynn

Musicians

Laura J Martin

Vidar Norheim

Company

Writer	**Jeff Young**
Director	**Serdar Bilis**
Designer	**Ti Green**
Composer and Sound Designer	**Martin Heslop**
Lighting Designer	**Chahine Yavroyan**
Video Designer	**Louis Price**
Movement Director	**Elinor Randle**
Dramaturg	**Lindsay Rodden**
Costume Supervisor	**Jacquie Davies**
Casting Director	**Kay Magson CDG**
Associate Lighting Designer	**Beky Stoddart**
Production Manager	**Jeff Salmon**
Company Manager	**Sarah Lewis**
Stage Manager	**Gemma Dunne**
Deputy Stage Manager	**Helen Lainsbury**
Assistant Stage Manager	**Gemma Gale**
Assistant Directors	**Joe Mellor (YEP, RTYDS), Cara Nolan (RADA)**
Lighting Programmer	**Andy Webster**
Sound No. 1	**Rob Newman**
AV Programmers	**Ian Davies** and **Jennifer Tallon-Cahill**
Automation Operator	**Mike Cantley**
Stage Crew	**Ricky Elliot**
Wardrobe Maintenance	**Tracey Johnson**
Dresser	**Sharona Prior**

The company would like to thank: The Royal Exchange Theatre Lighting Department

Cast

CARL AU
Alan 'Icarus'
Flynn

**PAUL
DUCKWORTH**
Lucas Firebright

Carl trained at Arts Ed.

Recent theatre include: *Jersey Boys* (Prince Edward Theatre); *Bells Are Ringing* (Union Theatre); *The Fantasticks* (Duchess Theatre, London); *A Christmas Carol* (Birmingham Rep); *Sleeping Beauty* (Oxford Playhouse); *High School Musical* (Hammersmith Apollo) and *Pendragon* (UK and Japanese tour with NYMT).

Television credits include: *Waterloo Road* (as series regular Barry) and *Casualty*.

Concerts include: *Barbara Cook and Friends* (London Coliseum) and *Good Thing Going* (Cadogan Hall).

Other credits include: Peter in *Peter and the Wolf* (Workshop – ACT Productions/Adam Cooper); *Flashdance* (Workshop); *Romeo and Juliet* (Workshop); *Dance: Radio* (Dry Write, York Theatre Royal, The Roundhouse, London); *Once Upon a Time at the Adelphi* (Workshop). Carl was also a featured dancer at the 2009 Brit awards.

In May 2007, Carl was the winner of the inaugural Stephen Sondheim prize for Student Performer of the Year.

Paul is one of Liverpool's most popular actors, with massive experience of both stage and screen.

Credits include: *Twelfth Night* (Liverpool Everyman); *Backbeat, Brookside, Little Scouse on the Prairie, Reds and Blues: The Ballad of Kenny and Dixie* and *Dreaming of a Barry White Christmas* (Echo Arena).

Paul has gained many plaudits recently for his role in *Beating Berlusconi*, a one-man show telling the tale of one Liverpool fan's experiences at Liverpool FC's legendary Istanbul Champions League Victory, and most recently has completed a successful run with Spike Theatre's anniversary production, *Sink or Swim*. He also appeared in the 10/10 acclaimed piece *Waiting for Brando* (Unity and National Tour) by Mike Morris and Steve Higginson, directed by Carl Cockram, in which he played (the controversial) 'Elia Kazan'.

He can be seen this Christmas at the BT Convention Centre Liverpool in *Dreaming of a Barry White Christmas*

RHIAN GREEN
The entire
population of
Lime Street

Theatre credits include: *Held* (Soho
Theatre Studio/Little London Theatre
Co.); *Tomorrow in the Battle*, rehearsed
reading (Roland Egan Productions);
Captain Oates' Left Sock (Finborough);
Duw a Ŵyr (Sherman Theatre); *The River*
(Ruth is Stranger than Richard); *Diwrnod
Dwynwen* (Sgript Cymru); *Pinocchio*
(Sherman Theatre) and *Woyzeck* (ELAN
Wales).

Television credits include: *Caerdydd,
Stick or Twist, A470, Tracy Beaker* and
Lucky Bag.

Film credits include: *A World After,
Aexis, Wrists, Y Lleill, The Tall Road to
Catrin Hogan, Meddwi* and *Diwrnod
Hollol Mindblowing Heddiw.*

Credits as director include: *A World
After, The Co-star* and *Too Late*.

PENNY LAYDEN
Lizzie Flynn

Theatre credits include: *Beryl* (West
Yorkshire Playhouse); *The Believers*
(Frantic Assembly); *Edward II, Table* and
Timon of Athens (National Theatre); *Nora*
(Coventry, Belgrade); *66 Books* (Bush
Theatre); *Incoming* (High Tide); *Lidless*
(Edinburgh & Trafalgar Studios); *Vernon
God Little* and *The Art of Random Whistling*
(Young Vic); *The Bacchae, Mary Barton,
Electra* and *Mayhem* (Manchester Royal
Exchange); *Comfort Me With Apples*
(Hampstead Theatre/Tour); *Dancing at
Lughnasa* (Birmingham Rep); *The Spanish
Tragedy* (Arcola); *Romeo and Juliet,
Helen, Hamlet* and *The Antipodes*
(Shakespeare's Globe); *Cinderella* (Old
Vic); *The Laramie Project* (Sound Theatre);
Assassins (Sheffield Crucible); *Popcorn*
and *Season's Greetings* (Liverpool
Playhouse); *The Tempest, Measure for
Measure* and *Roberto Zucco* (Royal
Shakespeare Company); *Jane Eyre, The
Magic Toyshop* and *A Passage To India*
(Shared Experience); *The Winter's Tale*
and *Ghosts* (Method & Madness); *What
I Did in the Holidays* (Cambridge Theatre
Company); *Maid Marion and Her Merry
Men* (Bristol Old Vic) and several seasons
in repertory at the New Vic, Stoke, under
the artistic directorship of Peter Cheeseman.

Television credits include: *Call the
Midwife, Prisoners' Wives, Land Girls,
Sirens, South Riding, Silent Witness, Poppy
Shakespeare, No Angels, The Bill, Bad
Mother's Handbook, Waterloo Road,
Murphy's Law, Doctors, Outlaws, M.I.T*
and *Casualty.*

Film credits include: *Broken* and *The
Libertine.*

Radio credits include: *Crime and
Punishment, Second Chance, Uganda* and
Return Ticket.

RHODRI MEILIR
Spike Smith

MARK RICE-OXLEY
Stephen Shakey

Rhodri studied Drama at Aberystwyth University, graduating in 2000. In 2014 he was awarded a Fellowship of the University. A lifelong Evertonian, he is delighted to be making his Liverpool debut with the Everyman.

Theatre credits include: *Mametz* (National Theatre Wales); *Gwlad yr Addewid* and *Dau.Un.Un.Dim/Yn y Tren* (Theatr Genedlaethol Cymru); *DJ Ffawst, Lysh, Ar y Lein, Y Wibdaith Wirion* and *Be o'dd enw ci Tintin?* (Theatr Bara Caws) and *Y Sgam, C'laen, Fala Surion* (Cwmni'r Fran Wen).

Television credits include: *Gwlad yr Astra Gwyn* (Rondo), *My Family, Doctors, Doctor Who* and *'Orrible* (BBC), *Y Pris, Pen Talar* and *Caerdydd* (Fiction Factory), *Afterlife* (Clerkenwell Films/ITV), *Rapsgaliwn* and *Teulu* (Boomerang), Terry Pratchett's *Hogfather* (Sky1), *A470, Pen Tennyn* (HTV) and *Tipyn o Stad* (Tonfedd Eryri).

Film and short film credits include: *Pride* (Pathe/BBC), *Under Milk Wood/Dan y Wenallt* and *The Circus/Y Syrcas* (Ffati Ffilms), *Mr Torquay's Holiday* (Trinder Films), *Patagonia* (Rainy Day Films), *Daddy's Girl* (Boda) and *The Baker* (Shakespeare's Cake), *Diwrnod Hollol Mindblowing Heddiw* (HTV), *Y Golau* (Opus), *Rapsgaliwn: Y Raplyfr Coll, Ble Mae Cyw?* (Boomerang) and *Neighbours* (NFTS).

Radio and Voiceover credits include: *It Ain't Over till the Bearded Lady Sings* and *Driving Home for Christmas* (BBC Radio 4), *Anturiaethau Aidan Mellberg, Llwch yn yr Haul* and *Enaid Hoff Cytun* (BBC Radio Cymru) and *Crwbanod Ninja* (Lefel 2).

Theatre credits include: *Playing with Grown Ups* (Brits Off Broadway); *Afraid of the Dark* (Charing Cross Theatre); *Tanzi Libre* (Southwark Playhouse); *Blood Brothers* (Phoenix Theatre, West End); *Town* (Royal and Derngate Theatres); *Switzerland* (High Tide Festival); *Much Ado About Nothing, Merchant of Venice* and *Holding Fire* (Shakespeare's Globe Theatre); *Pool (No Water)* (Frantic Assembly); *The Romans in Britain* (Crucible Sheffield); *The Life of Galileo* (Birmingham Rep Theatre); *David Copperfield* (West Yorkshire Playhouse); *The Kindness of Strangers* (Liverpool Everyman); *The Entertainer* (Liverpool Playhouse); *The Comedy of Errors* (Bristol Old Vic); *Cuckoos* (Barbican); *The Dwarfs* (Tricycle Theatre); *Workers Writes* (Royal Court Theatre) and *The Danny Crowe Show* (Bush Theatre).

Television credits include: *Whitechapel, WPC 56, Doctors, Preston Passion, Land Girls, New Tricks, Hotel Babylon, EastEnders, Holby City, The Dwarfs, Mersey Beat, Judge John Deed, In Deep, Two Pints of Lager and a Packet of Crisps.*

Film credits include: *The John Lennon Story.*

Radio credits include: *Four for a Boy, The Rake's Progress, A Helping Hand* and *Kaleido* by Jeff Young.

CATHY TYSON
Elsie Barmaid

KEIRAN URQUHART
Calumn Flynn

Cathy began her career at the Everyman Theatre and is delighted to be back for *Bright Phoenix*.

Theatre credits include: *Golden Girls* (Royal Shakespeare Company); *The Taming of the Shrew* (Regent's Park Open Air Theatre); *The Merchant of Venice* (Birmingham Rep); *Pygmalion* and *Educating Rita* (Theatr Clywd); *The May Queen* (Liverpool Everyman); *Burned to Nothing* (Tiata Fahodzi); *Stand* (Oxford Playhouse, Goode & Co) and *Mum's the Word* (Albery Theatre, West End).

Television credits include: *Coming Up: Hooked, Band of Gold, Scully, Always and Everyone, Night and Day, Emmerdale, Grange Hill, M.I.T., Doctors, Bonkers, A Thing Called Love, The Liverpool Nativity, Perfect* and *Rules of Engagement*.

Film credits include: *Mona Lisa, Priest, The Lost Language of Cranes, The Old Man Who Read Love Stories, Chick Lit, Business as Usual* and *Ollie Kepler's Expanding World*.

Cathy is the Winner of the Los Angeles Film Critics Award for Best Supporting Actress for *Mona Lisa*, and was nominated for the BAFTA Best Actress in a Leading Role, nominated for the Golden Globe's Best Supporting Actress for *Mona Lisa*.

Kieran is currently a drama student at The City of Liverpool College and after already studying Level 3 drama for a year is now going into his first year of HNC Drama studies.

Theatre credits whilst in college: FMP (Final Major Performance); *How to Disappear Completely and Never Be Found* by Fin Kennedy and *Benefit Street* – devised and directed by Tim Lynsky.

Kieran is also a young actor for the Young Everyman and Playhouse (YEP), where he made his stage debut performance in *The Grid* at the Everyman Theatre.

Kieran has just returned from touring an open-air production of *Jason and the Argonauts* with Off the Ground Theatre Company. This was his first professional theatre credit, touring nationally and internationally.

Kieran is excited to be working with the *Bright Phoenix* company.

Musicians

LAURA J. MARTIN

VIDAR NORHEIM

Liverpool's Laura J. Martin is a multi-instrumentalist songwriter, playing a long list of instruments: the flute, piano, mandolin, ukulele, harmonium etc. Laura is known by BBC 6 Music's Marc Riley as the 'Flute Wrangler'.

Her debut album, *The Hangman Tree* (Static Caravan, January 2012) received widespread acclaim, radio sessions (Marc Riley, Cerys Matthews, Lauren Laverne, Rob Da Bank) and higher profile gigs. Described as 'a musician of startling originality' by the *Sunday Times*, Laura has performed at many UK and European festivals (Greenman, Bestival, Soundwave, Reykjavik Music Mess).

The *Bónus Skór* EP followed in September 2012 and showcased an atmospheric soundscape influenced by the surroundings of the Icelandic recording sessions. Laura's latest album, *Dazzle Days* (November 2013), expands on the experience of soundtrack work for the BFI with more detailed arrangements and production touches. A favourite of BBC Radio 3's *Late Junction*, recording a live session for Max Reinhart at BBC Maida Vale, she has also appeared on *The Verb* with Ian McMillan, Benjamin Zephaniah and Michael Morpurgo. Laura will travel to Tokyo in November 2014 after being selected as one of 60 musicians to participate in the Red Bull Music Academy, Tokyo.

Vidar Norheim is a multi-instrumentalist, composer and producer originally from Norway. He studied BA Music at Liverpool Institute of Performing Arts. Vidar has toured worldwide as a member of Liverpool's alt pop unit Wave Machines, and worked extensively in a folk duo with Lizzie Nunnery. In 2011 he was named as Norway's most promising song writing talent, winning a place at Song:Expo in Trondheim alongside many of the world's leading songwriters and producers. Vidar also worked on projects with Willy Russell, Tim Firth and Frank Cottrell Boyce.

His theatre credits as composer and sound designer include: *Cheer Up*, *This is Only the Beginning* (Liverpool Playhouse); *100 Seel Street* (site specific); *Cartographers* (Theatre by the Lake) and *Pages from My Songbook* (Royal Exchange Theatre).

Radio and TV composition credits include: *The Singer*, an afternoon play for BBC Radio 4 and *Monkey Love*, a Three Minute Wonder for Channel 4.

Company

JEFF YOUNG
Writer

Jeff Young lives in Liverpool and has been writing for nearly 30 years. His work includes 35 radio plays, including four autobiographical drama documentaries and the site-specific drama documentary *Carandiru*, recorded in a prison in San Paulo, Brazil. He has been nominated for Prix Europa, Prix Italia and Sony Radio Awards. Jeff works in collaboration with artists, musicians, choreographers and film makers. His work has been performed in a drained submarine dock, a disused power station, parks, gardens, a derelict school, billboards, a bus station in Holland, ferry terminals and haunted buildings.

TV work includes: BBC dramas *EastEnders*, *Doctors*, *Casualty* and *Holby City*. His CBBC children's drama *Download* was part of the RTS North award-winning series *Stepping Up*.

In theatre Jeff's magical and poetic work has been produced by Bristol Old Vic, Northern Stage, Kaboodle, Kneehigh, Liverpool Everyman and Unity and many other theatres. He has worked in opera, puppet theatre, site specific and installation, public art projects, lantern parades, musicals, poetry, sound art and spoken word.

Over a period of ten years Jeff worked on a variety of projects with Pete Townshend from The Who, including *Lifehouse*, a Radio 3 drama, book and multi-CD archive, and a touring version of *Quadrophenia*.

His film *The Don* is scheduled to be filmed in 2015, directed by Marc Munden. He is currently writing a 5-episode radio adaptation of Jennifer Clement's book *Prayers for the Stolen* about the hundreds of young women kidnapped each year by Mexican drugs cartels.

SERDAR BILIS
Director

Theatre credits include: *Billy Wonderful* and *The May Queen* (Liverpool Everyman); *Proper Clever* (Liverpool Playhouse); *War* (Purtelas Theatre); *Lear*, *A Midsummer Night's Dream* and *Cloud Nine* (Sahne Kadir Has Istanbul); *Curse of the Starving Class* (Eskisehir Municipal Theatre); *Black Comedy* (Kocaeli Municipal Theatre); *Firtina/Tempest* (Istanbul International Theatre Festival) and *Knives in Hens*, *A Family Affair*, *Tartuffe* and *Night Just Before the Forests* (Arcola Theatre).

TI GREEN
Designer

Theatre credits include: *Romeo and Juliet* (HOME, Victoria Baths Manchester); *Woman in Mind* (Dundee Rep and Birmingham Rep); *Orlando* (Royal Exchange, Manchester); *A Christmas Carol* (Birmingham Rep); *Alice in Wonderland* (Polka Theatre); *Henry VI* (Shakespeare's Globe); *A Midsummer Night's Dream* (Royal & Derngate); *Time and the Conways* (Edinburgh Lyceum and Dundee Rep); *Unleashed* (Barbican/Blue Boy Entertainment); *DeadKidSongs*, *The Double and the Welsh Boy* (Theatre Royal, Bath); *The Tempest* (Dundee Rep); *Richard III* (Royal Shakespeare Company); *The Resistible Rise of Arturo Ui* (Liverpool Playhouse); *The Phoenix of Madrid*, *Iphigenia* and

The Surprise of Love (Ustinov Studio, Theatre Royal Bath); *Little Eagles* (Royal Shakespeare Company); *The Overcoat* (Gecko); *Liberty* (The Globe); *The Revenger's Tragedy* (National Theatre); *The Resistible Rise of Arturo Ui* (Lyric Hammersmith); *King Cotton* (The Lowry, Salford); *The Five Wives of Maurice Pinder* (National Theatre); *Coram Boy* (Imperial Theatre, New York, and Olivier, National Theatre); *The Hound of the Baskervilles* (West Yorkshire Playhouse); *The Ramayana* (Lyric Hammersmith); *Separate Tables* (Royal Exchange Theatre, Manchester); *Sante* (LSO St Luke's and Aldeburgh); *Tamburlaine* (Bristol Old Vic and Barbican); *The UN Inspector* (National Theatre); *The World Cup Final 1966* (Battersea Arts Centre); *Julius Caesar* (Royal Shakespeare Company); *Compact Failure* (Cleanbreak); *Paradise Lost* (Bristol Old Vic); *The Entertainer* (Liverpool Everyman); *The Comedy of Errors* (Bristol Old Vic); *Food Chain* (Royal Court); *Dimetos* (The Gate); *Where There's a Will* (Theatre Royal Bath tour) and *Coriolanus* (Royal Shakespeare Company, regional and US tour, Old Vic, London).

www.tigreen.net

MARTIN HESLOP
Composer and Sound Designer

Martin is a composer, sound artist and writer, originally from Northumberland and now living in Liverpool. He is a regular collaborator with Jeff Young and together they have worked on many projects including *Sputnik Jesus*, a live performance in the Radio City Tower, *The Curfew Tower Fragments* for the Curfew Tower LP, and an ongoing project *London Road* with artist Alan Dunn.

Martin has collaborated across art forms as a writer, poet, composer and musician, for performance, publications and visual art. He is currently artist-in-residence at arts organisation Metal.

His work for theatre has included text and music for *Cartographers* (Theatre by the Lake, Keswick); *Radical City* (Liverpool Everyman); *Stories in the Walls* (UnConvention Tyneside) and *Narvik* (Box of Tricks/Liverpool Everyman). He has also written for site-specific shows in places such as a thirteenth-century tower in Newcastle's city walls, Chester Castle and St George's Hall. His theatre work as a sound designer includes *Scarberia* (York Theatre Royal).

He recently composed the sound track to *Spider-Web City*, a short film which premiered at Uncharted Festival, Albania.

CHAHINE YAVROYAN
Lighting Designer

Theatre credits include: *Punk Rock* (The Lyric, Belfast); *Juvenalia, Dr Marigold and Mr Chops* and *Tuesdays at Tesco's* (Assembly Rooms); *Khandan* (Birmingham Rep/Royal Court); *The Pass, Let the Right One In, Narrative, Get Santa, Wig Out!, Relocated, The Lying Kind, Almost Nothing, At the Table, Bazaar* and *Another Year Wasted* (Royal Court); *King Lear, The House* and *Major Barbara* (Abbey, Dublin); *A Soldier in Every Son, Measure For Measure, Marat/Sade, Dunsinane, Elizabeth Gordon Quinn, Caledonia, Realism* and *The Wonderful World Of Dissocia* (National Theatre Scotland); *God In Ruins* and *Little Eagles* (Royal Shakespeare Company); *Farewell* and *Half a Glass of Water* (Field Day); *Uncle Vanya* (Minerva); *The Lady* *from the Sea*, *The Comedy of Errors* and *Three Sisters* (Royal Exchange, Manchester); *The Vortex* (Gate, Dublin); *Scorched* (Old Vic Tunnels); *Fuente Ovejuna, Punishment Without Revenge and Dr Faustus* (Madrid); *Orphans, Dallas Sweetman* and *Long Time Dead* (Paines Plough); *Jane Eyre* and *Someone Who'll Watch over Me* (Perth); *Il Tempo Del Postino* (Manchester International Festival) and *How to Live* (Barbican).

Dance credits include: *Jasmin Vardimon Dance, Bock and Vincenzi, Fraule Requardt, Colin Poole, Candoco, Ricochet, Rosemary Lee* and *Arthur Pita.*

Music work includes: *XX Scharnhorst* (HMS Belfast); *Sevastopol, Home* and *Dalston Songs* (ROH2); *Plague Songs* (Barbican); *The Death of Klinghoffer* (Scottish Opera); *Jocelyn Pook Ensemble* and *Diamanda Galas* (International).

Site-Specific Work: *Focal Point* (Rochester Harbour); *Enchanted Parks* (Newcastle); *Dreams of a Winter Night* (Belsay Hall); *Deep End* (Marshall St Baths) and *Ghost Sonata* (Sefton Park, Palmhouse).

Chahine Yavroyan is a longstanding People Show person.

LOUIS PRICE
Video Designer

Louis graduated from Central St Martin's School of Art. He is a director, editor and producer of films and documentaries, and also creates video imagery for theatre, dance and opera productions.

Louis is a director of November Films: www.novemberfilms.co.uk.

Recent video designs include: *Orango* (RFH, and 2014 tour, Helsinki and Stockholm Baltic Sea Festival); *Amphytrion* (Schauspielhaus Graz); *Unleashed* (Barbican Theatre); *The Resistible Rise of Arturo Ui* (Liverpool Playhouse); *The Ballad of the Sad Café* (Moulins des Paillard); *Five Soldiers*, interactive film (RKDC/ DCD installed at the Stadtmuseum, Dresden); *Beside the Sea* (Purcell Room, South Bank Centre); *Wings of Desire* (IDFB/Circa); *There Is Hope* (RKDC UK Tour) and *Sluts of Possession* which premiered in Holland, and the Edinburgh Festival in 2013.

He recently edited the feature film *In Mid Wickedness* (Tbilisi International Film Festival) and curated the video elements of the Young Vic Patrice Chereau tribute. Louis' short film collaboration with director William Oldroyd, *Best*, was selected in competition at the 2014 Sundance Film Festival. For November Films, as director: *Beyond Biba – A Portrait of Barbara Hulanicki* (SkyArts/ Sundance Channel) and *A Very British Cult* (in development with November Films/BBC Wonderland).

ELINOR RANDLE
Movement Director

Elinor is Artistic Director of Tmesis Theatre and Physical Fest (Liverpool's International Physical Theatre Festival). She is also a performer, choreographer director, lecturer and movement director.

Elinor studied drama at Liverpool John Moores University and has completed Hope Street's Physical Theatre Programme, where she developed a passion for movement and formed Tmesis theatre. Over the past ten years the company has developed a reputation, touring nationally and internationally, receiving critical acclaim for their unique style of movement based theatre, as well as their development of physical theatre in the northwest through Physical Fest.

www.tmesistheatre.com

LINDSAY RODDEN
Dramaturg

Lindsay is the Literary Associate for the Everyman & Playhouse, and runs the Playwrights' Programme, Everyword Festival and the theatres' work with writers both new and established.

She is also the dramaturg on many of the theatres' productions, most recently *Hope Place* (Everyman), *Scrappers* and *Held* (Playhouse Studio). Other recent work as a dramaturg has included *Cartographers* (Theatre by the Lake) and *My Life in Dresses* (Project Arts Centre, Dublin/national tour).

Recent writing includes: *Cartographers*; work with playwrights' collective Agent 160 including *A Modest Proposal* (Theatre 503, The Arches and Chapter Arts Centre) and *Sunday Morning, Dandelion Seeds* (Fun Palaces, Wales Millennium Centre); *Man With Bicycle, '73* and *Writing in the Dark* (The Miniaturists) and *The Almond Tree* (State of Wonder). She was invited to join the Royal Court's inaugural National Writers' Group in 2013.

Lindsay founded Almanac in 2010 with playwright/songwriter Lizzie Nunnery, producing, directing and writing adventurous collaborations with writers, musicians and other artists and theatre makers.

JACQUIE DAVIES
Costume Supervisor

Theatre credits include: *Juno and the Paycock, A View from the Bridge, Aladdin, A Day in the Death of Joe Egg, The Misanthrope, Jack and the Beanstalk, The Alchemist, The Norman Conquests, A Streetcar Named Desire, Cinderella, The Resistible Rise of Arturo Ui, Oedipus, Canary, Ghost Stories, The Hypochondriac, The Price, Our Country's Good, Tartuffe* and *Once Upon a Time at the Adelphi* (Liverpool Playhouse); *Scrappers, Held, The Match Box* (Liverpool Playhouse Studio); *Dead Dog in a Suitcase, Hope Place, Twelfth Night, Macbeth, Dead Heavy Fantastic, Sleeping Beauty, 'Tis Pity She's a Whore, Anthology, The Ragged Trousered Philanthropists, Dick Whittington, The Caretaker, Lost Monsters, Billy Wonderful, Mother Goose, Endgame, Eric's, Intemperance, The Way Home, The Morris* and *Port Authority* (Liverpool Everyman); *Vurt, Wise Guys, Unsuitable Girls* and *Perfect* (Contact Theatre, Manchester); *Oleanna* and *Memory* (Clwyd Theatr Cymru); *Love on the Dole* (The Lowry, Manchester); *Never the Sinner* (Library Theatre, Manchester) and *Shockheaded Peter* (West End).

Opera credits include work at: Scottish Opera, Buxton Opera Festival, Music Theatre Wales and Opera Holland Park.

Television and film credits include: *Queer As Folk*, *The Parole Officer*, *I Love the 1970s* and *1980s*, *Brookside* and *Hollyoaks*.

Design credits include: *Kes*, *Saturday, Sunday, Monday*, *Oh What a Lovely War*, *Into the Woods*, *The Rover*, *Titus Andronicus*, *Pericles*, *Spring Awakening*, *Twelfth Night*, *Macbeth*, *The Red Balloon*, *The Weirdstone of Brisingamen*, *Perfect*, *The Cherry Orchard*, *Machinal* and *Trelawny of the 'Wells'*.

JOE MELLOR
Assistant Director

Joe is a director currently on attachment at the Liverpool Everyman & Playhouse as part of the Regional Young Theatre Director Scheme.

Theatre credits include: *Arthur and Esther* (EV1 Studio, Liverpool Everyman); *Snowangel* and *Hand Over Fist* (Kings Arms Theatre); *Babel* (Lowry Studio); *Celebrity Death Pool* (Contact Theatre); *Breathing Corpses* (Victoria Baths) and *Lucky Dog* (John Thaw Studio).

Theatre credits as assistant director include: *The Widowing of Mrs Holroyd* (New Vic Theatre).

Joe is also Creative Founder of Fresh Loaf Productions.

CARA NOLAN
Assistant Director

Cara is currently studying on the MA in Theatre Directing at RADA.

Theatre credits include: *Yard Gal* and *The Wing* (RADA); *Oedipus* (Messini, Greece); *My Mother Said I Never Should* (Derby Theatre Studio); *Robin Hood and his Very Merry Men* (national tour); *Treasure Island* (national tour) and *Not So Grimm Fairy Tales* (national tour).

Theatre credits as assistant director include: *The Raft of the Medusa* and *The Witch of Edmonton* (RADA) and *The Tempest* (Derby Theatre).

Thanks to
Amy and Pearl,
Lindsay Rodden
and the Youngs and Petriccas

For Maureen Young
who took me to the pictures.

Bright Phoenix

'. . . the end of innocence, the darkness
of man's heart, and the fall through the air
of the true, wise friend . . . '

William Golding, *Lord of the Flies*

Author's Note

Bright Phoenix takes place mainly in the derelict Futurist cinema on Liverpool's Lime Street. Other locations such as Lime Street, the canal, rooftops and even the sky are part of the 'dream-world' of the play.

The story is set in the 1980s and the near enough present day. The scenes in the 1980s are hallucination memories that co-exist in time with the present day – it's just that sometimes the veneer between the past and present is thinner.

The musicians on stage are friends of the gang, always playing in the moment. The 1980s scenes are soundtracked by the musicians as if they are responding to the story they are witnessing – as if they are playing this music for the very first time, in response to the action. In the present day the musicians are playing, rehearsing, gigging. Whenever seems natural the actors and musicians should acknowledge each other because they inhabit the same world.

Take it for granted that booze and rubbish food are being consumed throughout. Lucas smokes, the rest of them are struggling to abstain. When Lucas lights up the others get a bit edgy, craving a smoke.

Les sanglots longs
Des violons
De l'automne
Blessent mon coeur
D'une langueur
Monotone

The long sobs
Of the violins
Of autumn
Wound my heart
With a monotonous
Languor

*This poem by Paul Verlaine was used to signal
to French Resistance fighters that they should
begin sabotage operations in the run-up to D Day.*

Characters

Lucy Jones, *Development Executive*

Elsie Barmaid
Lucas Firebright
Lizzie Flynn
Calumn Flynn
Alan 'Icarus' Flynn
Stephen Shakey
Spike Smith

Migsy
Val
Audrey
Pete the Piss
Maggie
Jimmy

The Entire Population of Lime Street

Scene One
THE AWKWARD BASTARDS

The present. Thursday night. 9 p.m.

*We hear before we see . . . the low-key hum and murmur of Lime Street at night when the drunks are rolling from bar to bar. Muted car horns and engines, sounds of drunken laughter and breaking glass, of distant karaoke singers and danger, of mystery and romance and drifting ghost whispers. Listen to the city, echoing through the night. It is ugly and beautiful and its noises seep into us. There is a woman – **Elsie** – floating and muttering . . .*

Elsie   Glory to them, one and all, glory to all of them, glory to me . . . Glory to the lot of us in the heart of all this glory . . .

*Drifting and twisting down the alleys there is the voice of a man – **Stephen** – singing in some accidental, harmony with the city. A woman – **Lizzie** – is hurrying through with bags of shopping, trying to flag down a taxi. She whistles.*

Lizzie   Taxi!

*She walks on. Down along the gutters, looking for dog-end fags, here comes **Spike**, wearing a heavy overcoat and hat with a patch over his left eye, muttering mad stuff out loud as he goes, dragging a crowbar which he scrapes and clatters against drainpipes, steel shutters and fire escapes.*

*He is drawn like a moth to the lights, to a Suit launching a Regeneration Project. **Spike** can't believe his luck. He saunters up to the TV presenter – **Lucy Jones** – who speaks through a microphone to camera.*

Lucy   . . . Only five minutes' walk from here this city's regeneration continues unabated. Meanwhile in Lime Street no one seems to have noticed . . . it's like a party in the ruins – an endless stag- and hen-night for Liverpool's disenfranchised, oblivious to this city's continuing renaissance . . .

Spike *is moving in for a closer, fascinated look.*

Lucy   Are these the people who will miss out on the rebranding of this city?

She turns to **Spike** *whom she is making feel uncomfortable, but he proceeds.*

Lucy   The city of Liverpool is being transformed –

Spike   Thank Christ! You saw it too? I thought it was only me who saw it happen . . .

Lucy *is unsettled but carries on.*

Lucy   – *transformed* by iconic developments defined by both leisure and business usage, which is a far cry from this madness . . .

Spike   Madness is right. It was earth-shattering. It ripped the night in two. I thought no one else had seen it but then Pete the Piss from the Yankee bar said he heard the noise – like screaming gods having their teeth pulled out is what he said – and he came running out the alehouse . . . and we fell down on our knees and tried to save them . . .

Lucy   Save them . . . ?

She is really unsettled now . . .

Spike   The night was what you might call *rent asunder* . . . I thought it was the death of us. There was nothing we could do . . . And so everything has changed now. And everything will be changed for ever. You talk about transformation. You talk about the city changing? Well, I'll tell you this, mate, last night was just the start because you've never seen a change like the change that's gonna come . . .

Spike *is thoroughly enjoying himself. And into Lime Street walks* **Lucas** *– battered leather jacket, fuck-off biker boots – lugging his bag as he leaves the train station, into the city. He stops and watches* **Spike** *with familiar amusement.*

Spike   The city ripped the length of Lime Street. Buildings fell. Drunks, dogs, mad bastards, taxis full of hen-nights, legless beggars . . . fell between the cracks into the guts of Liverpool . . .

And I lay down in the gutter and cried, O earth why do you split open? And hurl into your gaping sewers great multitudes of men!

Lucas *watches, impressed. Nods . . .*

Spike   Down there. Down that grid. Eyeless souls, mongrels . . .

Now **Elsie** *is drawn like a moth towards them until* **Lucy** *is feeling hemmed in.*

Spike (*suddenly nicely*)   Is this the sort of thing you're thinking of?

Lucy *brazens it out, nervously addressing the camera.*

Lucy   Is it people like this poor soul who will miss the chance to participate in *the vision* as we walk into the stimulating, bright, new morning of this city . . . ?

Spike *falls down on his knees and starts crowbarring the grid out of the gutter. As he heaves at the grid he spits at* **Lucy.**

Spike   What about the awkward bastards?

Lucy   Excuse me?

Spike   The awkward bastards like me who don't want to go?

Lucy   Have you *seen* the brochure? You'll all want to go . . .

Spike   I don't. Listen to the laughter. Listen to the songs! Listen to the lovely drunkards singing down there in the bowels of the earth . . .

He shouts into the drain.

Spike   It's OK! The night will come! You drunken men, you dogs, you legless beggars and you perfumed saints . . . the night will come when you will re-emerge in swarms of bugs and roaches and once you've read the brochure . . .

He sticks his hand in the drain. Sticks his head in.

Lucy   Surely you don't want to stay here?

Spike (*popping his head out*)   What's wrong with here?

Lucy *looks around in disbelief. Looks for back-up. Doesn't get any.*
Spike *gets up. The hand he stuck into the drain is bleeding but he doesn't notice.*

Lucy   Well . . . the noise. The *people* . . . why would anyone in their right mind want to stay here?

Spike   Because we've spent our lives here . . .

This isn't what **Lucy***'s after.*

Lucy   Take him out! Get him out of here!

But **Spike** *carries on.*

Spike   . . . Between two pubs. Gin palaces. Ballrooms. Weddings, funerals and christenings. First kiss and famous last words. This is where the magic is. This is where the night makes everyone look beautiful . . .

Lucas *moves in. He takes out a tobacco pouch and rolls a cigarette. He nods, smiles in approval.*

Lucas   On streets where we've fallen in and out of love. In cinema queues. And dancing. Dancing in the rain.

Spike *looks at* **Lucas** *as if he's only just noticed him. He looks him up and down, weighs him up, smiles his broken, brown-toothed smile.*

Spike   Exactly. What are you gonna do about people like us who like dancing in the rain?

Lucy *winces, searches for the words, tries some for size.*

Lucy   The regeneration brochure has a chapter on leisure . . .

Spike   When your bright happy tomorrow comes are you gonna look around thinking – 'Oh, that's a shame, that mad bastard with one eye hasn't turned up. He's missing out on our bright happy tomorrow . . . ' I couldn't give a shite about your . . .

He looks to **Lucas** *for help.*

Lucas   Try, mirage of lies . . .

Spike *turns to* **Lucy**, *who can't look him in the eye.*

Spike   Exactly! Mirage of lies. Well, you know what, mate? In all honesty, if I can find a bigger grid than this, I'm going down there with the wild beasts.

The world changed in the dark hours and let me tell you this . . . if it comes like a blizzard or comes like a firestorm, when the scar in the gutter splits open and the drunks and dogs come pouring out, however it comes, we'll have no need of your shiny, bright tomorrow!

He sticks his head down the drain and shouts to the trapped souls. And then he notices his bleeding hand . . .

Spike   Oh bollocks, look at me hand.

He shows **Lucy** *the palm of his scratched and bloody hand.*

Lucy   You're bleeding . . .

Spike   Yeah. Must have been a mad dog, down there in the sewers . . .

Lucy   You need help.

Spike   So help me. Touch me. Take me in your arms.

Lucy   What?

Spike   Take me in your arms and love me. Show me that you love me. Go on.

Lucy   I meant you need help. (*Taps head.*) Serious help.

Spike   Come on . . . just take me in your arms. Rock me a little while. Show me that you're able. Rock me like a helpless child. In a cradle.

A pause. **Lucas** *watches* **Spike**, *shaking his head in wonder as* **Spike** *offers himself to* **Lucy**, *who recoils.*

Spike   Nah . . . thought not. Fuck you! Fuck you and your business!

Lucy *just watches him in slack-jawed silence as* **Spike** *comes to a stuttering halt, swaying, subsiding. Sudden silence. Then nice as pie.*

Spike   Anyway. Nice meeting you.

He takes hold of **Lucy**'s *hand and shakes it as if they've just taken afternoon tea together.* **Lucy** *just looks at his hand, covered in* **Spike**'s *blood. And she turns back to camera. As she backs away planning a new career,* **Spike** *walks happily away. He suddenly stops, face to face with* **Lucas**.

Lucas   Hello, Spike. Long time no see.

Spike *pretends he's not sure who* **Lucas** *is.* **Lucas** *offers him a smoke. He takes it, lighting it with* **Lucas**'s.

Spike   Sorry . . . ?

Lucas   It's me. Lucas . . .

Spike *laughs, blows smoke into* **Lucas**'s *face.*

Spike   I know it's Lucas! Same old leather jacket! Still the cool bastard. Must be twenty years. How you doing?

Lucas   Not bad, yeah. How's the old . . .

He points at **Spike**'s *eye patch.* **Spike** *fishes around in his overcoat pocket and pulls out a glass eye. Offers it to* **Lucas** *who recoils but accepts it when* **Spike** *insists.* **Spike** *flips up his eye patch and shoves his face in* **Lucas**'s, *making him look at the empty eye-socket.*

Spike   Can you see? Can you see, Lucas? Cos I can't see.

Lucas   I know.

Spike *shoves him again.* **Lucas** *holds out the eye.* **Spike** *snatches it from his shaking hand.*

Spike   Open your mouth.

Lucas   Is this a joke?

Spike   Open your bloody mouth.

Lucas *doesn't know what else to do.* **Spike** *grabs his face by the jaw and shoves the glass eye in* **Lucas**'s *mouth.*

Spike   Swallow it. Go on, swallow it.

Lucas *swallows the eye in horror as* **Spike** *stands there laughing his head off.*

Spike   Now we're even. I've lost one eye, it's unlikely I'll lose another. You my friend are now – temporarily – packing a spare!

He does a dance of joy, suddenly stops. **Lucas** *laughs.*

Lucas   You're mad as you ever were.

Spike   No I'm not. I'm madder!

Lucas   All that stuff you just made up? All that shit about men and dogs falling into the bowels of the earth.

Spike   I never made it up. It really happened. Pint?

Then he walks off dragging his crowbar in his bleeding hand, leaving **Lucas** *standing there, stunned.*

Scene Two
WHERE TROUBLE MELTS LIKE LEMON DROPS

The present. Thursday night. A little later.

A beautiful voice – **Stephen***'s – echoes through the city, a strange serenade, as if sung by a cabaret angel.*

ROOFTOP LOVESONG

Stephen
    She's not a mimic or a pawn
    She's the writer of the rules
    She paints her lips with brick-dust
    And she dresses under moons

    Her eyes are ringed in coal soot
    A chimney neck of pearls
    And she's more than we can know
    And she's more than we deserve

And oh she conducts
Till the night does obey
And sends all our worries to the sea
A tangle of nylon
A cracked leather swag
And her heels dance the rain
And we rise from the cracks
And swing from her curls
Carving carousel whirls

Elsie *dances, half singing along, murmuring men's names in the gutter.*

Elsie   Arthur . . . Billy . . . boy . . . boy . . . touch me, touch me gently . . . Take me to the dancing days and waltz me round the hall, hold me tight and hold me tender, in between your strong arms, let me feel your heartbeat beating, taste your salt on my sweet lips. Love me amongst the glow worms, moon moths and insects like the GI Joe who loved me in the roses long ago . . . the man who laddered my silk stockings in the rough and lusty tumble . . .

She becomes unsettled by noises. Her reverie falls away from her and the night is no longer sensual; it is a place that makes her feel afraid.

Listen to the broken-winged night-bird singing to an orchestra of ambulances and fire alarms . . .

Don't leave me in the darkness, please don't leave me aching, I can't bear the ache of loneliness in the darkness all alone . . . Don't leave my heart in pieces in the broken glass and gutters . . . Don't leave me torn and tattered in the city full of fear . . .

She holds herself. The night goes on around her.

As **Elsie** *looks to the night she holds her fears inside herself as* **Lucas** *and* **Spike** *walk down an alley.* **Spike** *reaches the bottom of a scaffolding ladder and starts to climb.*

Spike   Come on, bollocks . . .

He gestures to **Lucas** *to follow him.* **Lucas** *climbs . . . The voice gets louder as they reach the top. And there they find* **Stephen**, *dressed like a diva, singing amidst the chimney pots and TV aerials.*

Lucas   Ste! It's me, Lucas!

Spike   Not now, Luke. Not while he's fluid . . .

He wraps his bleeding hand in gaffer tape and passes **Lucas** *a can of beer. They sit on the edge of the roof, open their beers and slug.*

Lucas   Heard this on the radio in a bar in Amsterdam! I'd forgotten how beautiful Ste sings . . .

Stephen *comes to the end of the song. He has seen* **Lucas** *but carries on as if he hasn't noticed him.*

Stephen   That song was for you, my city, so beautiful in the night, your face carved with stories and teardrops of rain.

Spike   That's lovely, that!

Stephen   Every night I climb up on to your rooftops and sing songs of broken-hearted love beneath the moon and stars –

Spike (*explaining to* **Lucas**)   He's sort of in love with the city.

Stephen   – gazing down at the beautiful women, all tottering heels and hair furniture . . . and the city is a menagerie. My secret world, up on the rooftops –

Spike (*explaining to* **Lucas**)   Like a night club in the sky!

Stephen   Up here I can get closer to the moon. Sing to the girls knocking off from their shift in the lap-dance bar and the women on the top decks of buses, weeping into tissues. This is my cabaret . . .

Up here I am the *moon crooner*!

And tonight a stranger came to town, a boy who ran away and left us long ago, slipping away through rainy streets and leaving love behind. Did the old town look the same when he stepped down from the train . . . ? And now that he's walked down Lime Street in his old home town, what is he feeling? What is he thinking?

Spike   He's thinking, how did I end up on a rooftop with a one-eyed nut-job and a bloke who sings to chimneys . . .

Lucas *lights up again. He isn't exactly comfortable with all this, but pretends otherwise.* **Spike** *loves this – laughing. He dangles his legs over the edge of the rooftop, drinking beer.*

Spike   Ah, priceless! Come and sit with us, Ste!

Stephen *stands, takes a fag off* **Lucas**, *wants to smoke it but gives it back, slightly holier-than-thou.* **Lucas** *looks at them, confused.*

Spike   Me and Ste are on a health-and-beauty kick . . .

Stephen
   'A cigarette that bears a lipstick's traces . . .
   These foolish things . . . '

Spike (*laughing*)   He's doing the lyric thing! I love it when he does the lyric thing. Smoking is bad for you, Luke. Our bodies are temples.

Lucas   His might be, but yours has been looted. Still singing then, Ste?

Stephen
   'Some day I'll wish upon a star,
   Wake up where the clouds are far behind me . . .
   Where troubles melt like lemon drops
   Away above the chimney-tops,
   That's where you'll find me . . . '

Lucas *looks at* **Stephen** *and then looks to* **Spike**, *a little bit bewildered by the whole thing.* **Stephen** *isn't making things easy for him.* **Spike** *is loving it.*

Spike   Your face, Luke! Ah, isn't this great? Ste's made up to see you.

Lucas   No he isn't! I wasn't expecting hugs and kisses . . .

Spike   Why not? I'll hug you.

He gives **Lucas** *a hug. They teeter on the edge of the roof.*

Spike   When you went off into the big wide world I went into the world of misdiagnosed mental disorders. Never stand on the edge of a rooftop with a one-eyed madman. Oh shit, too late!

Lucas   Ah Spike, you never stood a chance . . .

Spike   I never had any illusions. Not like you and your romantic notions.

Lucas   All I ever wanted was to be where the action was. Paris, Amsterdam . . .

Stephen   You missed out on Liverpool's 'Cultural Renaissance'.

Spike   Is right. You can get a pint of smoothflow in Smokey Mo's at half eight in the morning now . . .

Stephen   And we've got cafés. Cafés with chairs outside! You don't get that in Paris.

A look of hurt and anger passes over his face as his true feelings come out.

But shitting hell, Lucas. You just . . . disappeared. I mean, twenty years?

Lucas   What can I say? While you two losers were pissing your lives away, while you were scratching on, I was driving from Morocco to Amsterdam with hubcaps full of the sweetest grass you've ever smoked in your dreams . . . squatting in old warehouses in the Red Light District . . . While you were working on the Christmas post, I was working in a travelling snake circus down in Acapulco and *canoodling* . . .

Spike   Canoodling!

Lucas   *Canoodling* with the ringmaster's missus on the sly . . . While you two were picking dog-ends from the gutter and dressing like your auntie, I was riding the Wall of Death on a customised Vincent Black Lightning, the length and breadth of Venezuela . . .

Spike   I heard you were washing dishes in Eastbourne.

Stephen   Didn't see you in Ibiza. I was in the vanguard, me. E'd off me face in Amnesia. No one turns a hair at a man in a floral frock in Playa d'en Bossa.

Lucas   I'm talking *proper* travelling . . . Deportation! Living.

Stephen   What makes you think we're interested?

Spike   I'm interested!

Lucas   Damn right you are, Spike! But you two? What have you been doing with your lives?

Spike   Well, in between being sectioned so many times I'm practically a member of staff, I've been . . .

He checks over his shoulders in case anyone is listening. He whispers.

I've been stealing the city.

Lucas *laughs.*

Spike   Straight up. Places are closing down all the time – community centres, boozers, libraries, swimming baths. And once a building's closed it dies before your eyes. Roof caves in, cellars flood, windows smash. And they wait. They wait so long that people forget the building's there. Knock it down, done for. Or turn it into luxury apartments. So I break in and anything that's not nailed down I take and weigh it in. I've grafted since I was a kid. For nothing. So, you know, keep the wolf from the door . . .

Lucas   The scrap man and the pop star!

Stephen   *Failed* pop star. I'm now a work of art. I get spat at, laughed at and battered. But I still have the golden voice. I wish upon a star and serenade the city from its rooftops. Tonight, I sing from on top of a lap-dancing bar . . .

Spike   The jewel in the crown of our cultural renaissance!

Stephen   Who knows where the phantom crooner will strike next! I am beautiful. The city is beautiful. Look at her!

They look out at the beautiful city and its twinkling lights. **Spike** *and* **Lucas** *raise and clink their beer cans, laughing.* **Stephen** *takes the microphone.*

Stephen   This song is for Boozie Dorothy on the top deck of the 82, heading home with hope in her dear heart . . .

And then he sings. His voice drifts and echoes across the rooftops and **Lucas** *looks in wonder as musicians emerge from the shadows and play along with* **Stephen** *while people dance in Lime Street.*

SKIN AND BONES

Stephen
    We're all made of skin and bones
    And rights and wrongs
    And when the lights are turned down low
    We all dance to the same old songs

    So keep winding your Wurlitzer baby
    This is no time to be moving along
    Keep pouring those pints of that strong red wine
    This is no time to be gone

    We all come from broken homes
    We all swear too much, don't go to church
    We work to pay the tolls
    So we can walk down the same old roads

    So keep winding your Wurlitzer baby
    This is no time to be moving along
    Keep pouring those pints of that strong red wine
    This is no time to be gone

And then the ghost of **Alan Icarus**, *dressed like a steampunk pilot, appears and only* **Lucas** *can see him.* **Spike** *laughs at* **Lucas**'*s face.*

Spike   I'm glad you came back.

Lucas   It was *time* to come back. You know . . . face the music.

He is still looking at **Alan Icarus** *drawing closer across the rooftops.*

Spike   Shit happens, mate. Just don't come back expecting party hats.

Lucas   What about Lizzie?

The ghost of **Alan Icarus** *is moving in closer.*

Spike   Aah! Here we go. This is why he's back! She won't see you.

Alan *is right up close but only* **Lucas** *is aware of his presence.*

Lucas   You could give me her number though? I could give her a ring . . . Come on, Spike!

Spike *laughs and raises his beer can. He leans over the edge and points down below with his crowbar.*

Spike   You'll find her down there. In the Futurist. Right, I'm off scrapping. You got yourself a place to stay?

Lucas   Yeah yeah. Don't worry about me . . . I'll be out and about. People to see, places to go . . .

Spike *studies him, nods.*

Spike   Is right. Take it easy, kid . . .

Alan *drifts away, softly singing 'Light up the Sky with Standard Fireworks'.* **Lucas** *hears it, not quite understanding. He climbs down the ladder as the song takes him back to the past.*

Scene Three
PILOT KINGDOM

The past. Daytime.

A hallucination is forming around **Lucas** *as he descends to the street. He is eight years old. He carries a wooden box – an antique crystal radio. Around his neck hangs a set of headphones. He sees the shell of a dead firework lying in the gutter. He picks it up and starts walking down the street picking up the shells of fireworks as he goes.*

Lucas (*singing*)
    'Light up the skt with Standard Fireworks . . . '

Alan Icarus, *about the same age, is walking towards him, wearing a flying jacket made out of a dressing gown, wellies, aviator goggles and a balaclava. He is carrying a paper aeroplane, which he 'flies', hand held above his head. He spots* **Lucas** *and he's pissed off.*

Alan   Hey! You!

Lucas *looks over his shoulder.*

Alan   I'm talking to you, soft lugs. What the bloody hell you doing in our kingdom?

Lucas   I'm just collecting dead fireworks . . .

Alan   Well, you'd better give 'em back cos the bloody things are ours.

Lucas *picks up a dead firework. Thrilled with the treasure, holds it up in awe.*

Lucas   It's a Bright Phoenix! Beats a Dazzler any day.

Alan *is pissed off, mixed with admiration.*

Alan   You jammy bastard!

Lucas   Why are you dressed like that?

Alan   I'm Icarus.

Lucas   What?

Alan   You don't know about Icarus?

Lucas (*affronted*)   Course I bloody know about Icarus!

Alan   Well then, you should know who I am. Only just landed, lucky to be alive.

Lucas *studies him doubtfully.*

Alan   Don't suppose you've got a smoke?

Lucas   I'm only eight.

Alan   I've been smoking since I was four and a half. What are you, one of them late-developers?

Lucas   I'm from down the alley.

Alan   Like I said, you're one of them late-developers.

Lucas   Stop being so bloody mean.

Alan *gets closer, studies him.*

Alan   Have you got your pilot's licence?

Lucas   I . . .

He doesn't know what to say.

Alan   It's just that me crate crash-landed in Stephen Shakey's yard and there's a bloody war on in case you hadn't noticed.

Lucas   Do you need some help?

Alan   Course I need some help. The heroes of British aviation are working round the clock to get my Lancaster bomber back up in the air and we need all the help we can get.

Lucas   I see . . .

Alan   So, how about it? Are you in?

Lucas *nods as* **Alan** *takes him by the hand and shakes it manfully. They start to walk.*

Alan   See any dog-ends, nab 'em.

And they walk down the street, picking up firework shells and dog-ends. They go through a backyard gate; inside there are two other boys 'fixing' a crashed aeroplane made from dustbins, stepladders, broomsticks, oil-drum lids and planks salvaged from dead houses, bin bags, dollies, planks, metal dustbin lids with metal handles, a broken fan, an umbrella 'propeller'.

Spike   You can be Douglas Bader, Ste . . .

Stephen   I don't want to be Douglas Bader, he's a dick . . .

On a tyre and rope swing there is a girl – **Lizzie**. **Lucas** *looks at her, she pulls a face, he looks away shyly. She's bloody gorgeous.*

The boys – **Stephen** *wearing a dress and* **Spike** *– stop working when they see the arrivals.* **Spike** *comes over, squares up to* **Lucas** *and shoves him hard in the chest.*

Spike   What are you doing here? Spy, are you?

Stephen (*calmly*)   We should execute him.

Lucas   What?

Stephen   For enemy activities.

He drags on a dog-end and blows smoke like a veteran. He nods to **Spike**.

Stephen   Kill him.

Alan *is in the middle of strapping on a pair of wings made from feathers and metal. He pauses.*

Alan   Ah, not again. You can't kill him!

Stephen (*shrugs*)   He knows too much already. Besides, I killed the last one. It's Spike's turn.

Alan *looks at* **Lucas**, *gives him a shrug of apology.*

Alan   Sorry, mate. It's just the way it is.

Lucas *tries to back away but* **Spike** *gets him by the collar and starts laying into him. He gets him to the ground and kicks him.* **Lucas** *just curls up in a ball, takes the kicking. Until . . .*

Lucas (*desperate*)   I've got an antique –

Stephen *climbs out of his bin and walks towards* **Lucas**, *signalling* **Spike** *to stop.*

Stephen   What?

Lucas (*looking up*)   Yeah, a crystal radio.

He holds the wooden box up for proof. **Stephen** *takes it off him.* **Spike** *starts kicking him again.*

Spike   You're a spy! (*Kicking.*) You rotten bastard.

Lizzie *climbs off the swing and goes over to the fracas.*

Lizzie   I reckon he could be useful to us. I reckon if he's got a radio set we could use it to send secrets. That's what I reckon.

Lucas   I reckon she's right. I know all kinds of brilliant stuff *and* I'm in the French Resistance. I can listen to stuff from all over the world and the mad thing is, it just looks like a box . . .

Stephen *pulls* **Spike** *off, kicks him in the pants and sends him skulking off. They all look at* **Lizzie**.

Lizzie   I reckon he looks interesting. If he was in a film at the pictures he'd be the one the girls are mad about.

They're fazed by this. Not sure where to look.

Alan   Ah, that's disgusting . . .

Stephen   Nah. If he was in a film he'd have a better quiff. The girl's'd only go for him if he had the proper hair.

Lizzie   My name's Lizzie. I'm gonna be a freedom-fighter in Bolivia . . .

Lucas   My name's Lucas.

Smiling shyly at each other.

Pleased to meet you . . . Lucas!

Spike   Oh stop it!

Alan (*to* **Lucas**)   Yeah, bloody stop it.

Stephen   Have you got evidence about Douglas Bader on your crystal radio?

Lucas, *still trying to work out what he's got himself into, nods. That's good enough for* **Stephen**.

Stephen   Good. Cos I bloody hate that Douglas Bader and his bloody stupid legs.

He pulls **Lucas** *to his feet.*

Stephen   This new boy's on the flight. Anyone who doesn't like that has me to answer to.

They all nod. **Lucas** *is looking at* **Stephen** *strangely.*

Stephen   What?

Lucas   Why are you wearing a dress?

Spike   He's wearing a dress because he hasn't made his mind up. Have you got a problem with that?

Lucas   No, not really.

Stephen (*threatening*)   Boy can't wear a dress?

Lucas   No, yeah, it's just . . .

Lizzie (*explaining*)   You see, we do our best to live in magical places. Do you live in magical places?

Lucas   Sorry?

Lizzie   Do you live in magical places like the cinema and bonfire night?

Lucas   Yes, I suppose I do . . .

Stephen   And the Wild West and the sky above and the dirty old canal?

Lucas   All the bloody time.

Stephen   Then come with us on a bombing raid.

Lizzie   Unless you're scared of flying?

Lucas   I'm not scared of anything.

Laughter. He's in.

What's the name of this outfit?

Spike (*proudly*)   We're called – (*French accent*) the Awkward Bastards!

*He shakes **Lucas**'s hand. **Stephen** climbs into his dustbin, takes hold of his yard-brush joystick and gives **Lucas** a once-over through his broken binoculars.*

Stephen   We'll talk about that legless Bader when we're back in the officers' mess . . .

*They all climb on board – into bins and boxes. They put on colander helmets and pick up walkie-talkies made from tin cans on string. **Alan** makes a few adjustments to his wings and dons his flying goggles. **Lizzie** climbs in next to **Lucas**, tapping his wooden box. He smiles at her shyly and puts on his headphones.*

Alan   Right, lick the battery.

*Alan takes out a battery and licks it, jumping slightly at the electric shock on his tongue. He passes the battery to **Stephen** who licks it and passes it to **Spike** who licks it and passes it to **Lizzie** who licks it and passes it to **Lucas** – who looks at it, confused.*

Alan   Lick it.

Lucas   I don't want to lick it.

Stephen   Lick the bloody battery or we'll definitely murder you.

Lizzie   It doesn't hurt. Just lick it.

Alan   We need the energy. We can't take off without it. If you're me mate? Be me mate and let's be heroes?

*Lucas shrugs and reluctantly licks it, with **Lizzie**'s smiling encouragement. He recoils at the shock.*

Lizzie   There! You've kind of kissed me now.

Spike   You've kind of kissed all of us!

*They collapse in laughter. **Alan** slaps **Lucas**'s back warmly. He takes out a stick-on moustache and slaps it on his upper lip. Salutes.*

Alan   Now we're full of battery juice and that means we can fly.

Stephen *taps the side of his dustbin and then starts vibrating. They all rattle and shake like maniacs as they set off,* **Spike** *pushing buttons over his head, keeping the crate on track . . .*

Stephen   Bumpy start . . . taxi-ing down the runway, me, the new boy, Spike, Lizzie and Icarus, the battered old bomber plane shaking . . . lifting from the ground . . .

They judder and shudder in their bins and boxes, as if they're hurtling down a runway and taking off into the sky.

(Into his tin-can walkie-talkie.) And in our dreams we are airborne, slipping the bonds of the earth, flying on a wing and a prayer over the rooftops of Liverpool, embracing the elemental eternity of heaven . . . ROGER. TEN FOUR. OVER AND OUT!

And in their imaginations they fly, the heavy rumble of bomber engines and music filling the air . . .

Scene Four
THE FUTURIST

The present. Friday morning.

A man – **Migsy** *– flogging knock-off goods weaves through the street.* **Lucas** *has been walking all night and is looking really rough.*

Migsy   Bin bags! Lighters five for a pound . . . Want any tobacco . . . Come on, ladies . . . ? Batteries? Gents' socks? What's wrong with yous? Here y'are love . . . Jesus, give a guy a chance . . . *(To* **Lucas**.*)* Socks, mate? Sweatless socks? You look like a man who sweats . . .

Lucas   I don't need sweatless socks . . .

Migsy *(affronted)*   We *all* need sweatless socks, mate. Even homeless losers like yourself.

It starts to rain. **Migsy** *takes out an umbrella.*

Migsy   Umbrellas! £2.99 your umbrellas!

Lucas *takes the umbrella and hands over three quid.* **Migsy** *hurries off smiling – another mug has parted with his money.*

Migsy   Gents' socks! Batteries! Where would the world be without sweatless socks and batteries? House in Toxteth, yours for a quid? Jesus tonight! Tight-fisted bastards . . .

He strides off, muttering about the state of the world, leaving **Lucas** *on the steps of the Futurist Cinema.* **Lucas** *puts the umbrella up. It's full of holes. He stands there in the rain. The ruined Futurist sign fizzes and flickers.*

Inside the Futurist, grown-up **Lizzie** *is in the rubble-strewn ruins, a beam of light shining through the broken roof illuminating her in the gloom. She is singing along to music – played by the musicians but seemingly coming out of a battered tape recorder.*

ROW ON

The Band
There goes the sky, spinning clouds
While I lie here watching the river flow
There goes her mouth, spitting memories to the sea
All is lilac and moon but my soul doesn't cast a shade
There's echoes in the silence, but they don't reach me
And the wind blows strong with that old sad song
Row on

I wanna go to where there's waterfalls and rocky crags
I'll cup my hands till they fill right up with rain
And in that soft meadow morning, I'll bathe in the willow
    grass
And dream that you hold me as the day rolls past
But I'll still sing along to that old sad song
Row on

Lizzie
Don't we all?
Oh that's just romance my love, this is the land of the real
And there's many voices calling but they shout from the
    underclass

They're chained to the metal that pays for their next meal
And we all beat along to that old slave song
Row on

Lucas *walks into the cinema towards her – not sure if it's her.* **Lizzie** *turns to a heap of junk – old paint tins, film stock, mangled metal, a cinema seat. She's uncoiling a cable and whipping it in the dust still singing along to the music.*

Lucas   Lizzie . . . ?

Lizzie *turns – first sighting of each other after all this time. She stops singing suddenly and the music stops with her. She lets the cable fall. Weighing up the changes in each other's faces.* **Lizzie** *picks up an old paint can and a stick and starts stirring and poking at the half-dry paint inside. She scoops up some dirt, throws it in the can, spits in the can, mixes and stirs.*

Lucas   What you doing?

Lizzie (*still stirring*)   Making a bomb.

He watches her in awkward silence as she stirs the paint can. There's a can of diesel on the heap. She pours it in and stirs. He watches hesitantly, not sure whether to stay or to walk away.

Lizzie   Changed a bit, hasn't it?

Lucas   I've always had this memory of me mam and me watching *Mickey's Christmas Carol* . . .

Lizzie   You never did that. You were always running wild and your mam was at home going mad.

Lucas   I was expecting to come here today and – you know – see the old velvet seats and the ice-cream girl.

Lizzie   No one needs a dirty old fleapit full of snotty kids and weeping mums. They kind of wiped the Futurist off the Things to See and Do list. They let it die.

And I'd walk past here every day, getting more and more pissed off and then one day I just thought – sod it – and I crowbarred me way in and starting bringing it back from the dead.

She sees by the way he looks at her that this sounds mad. She runs her hand through her hair . . .

Don't know why. You know me, like a fight . . .

They don't know what to say. Awkward. To fill the silence he tells a story . . .

Lucas Ever tell you about my granddad? He was the only man in history to drown inside a cinema. Straight up. He sat there – (*Points.*) Row D, Seat 46, bit drunk, fell asleep, slept right through a storm, rain pouring in through the roof like the tropics. Devastation. They found him dead, drowned, smiling, eyes open, still watching the film. What was he watching?

Lizzie *Singing in the Rain!* Piss off!

Lucas True story.

Lizzie You haven't changed. Still full of crap. Still wearing that smelly old leather.

He looks at his jacket. He thought it was cool . . .

You look bloody awful.

Lucas Been walking all the night . . .

Lizzie I wish you hadn't come . . .

Lucas Yeah, well . . . I just had to come. I had to find out. You look . . .

Lizzie You know what? Things are all right for me. I've got stuff in my life . . .

Lucas Me too . . .

Lizzie You're lying. You've got nothing. I can tell . . .

Lucas Maybe that's why I came back. There I was dodging the narcotraficantes in Colombia . . .

Lizzie Yeah, right . . .

Lucas Tilting at windmills in Andalucia . . . riding the rails to Santa Fe with dustbowl ghosts . . .

Lizzie Bollocks!

Lucas And I thought, time to go home. Hook up with the gang. And Lizzie. See if Lizzie's alive and kicking and if she's beautiful still.

Lizzie Don't tell me you came back here for me! I didn't even notice you'd gone.

Lucas You did!

Lizzie Nah. Been too busy. I *was* going to Bolivia. As planned. But I had to live for too many years with a twat who turned out to be a scuzzbag dealer, and by the time I'd got rid of him the Revolutionary Liberation Movement had gone a bit pear-shaped. Then there was the rent strike and organising various sit-ins and, oh yeah, taking your dad pans of scouse up until his miserable death. Oh, all kinds of stuff. And my son.

Lucas Son?

Lizzie Not now. Not now.

Lucas I wasn't even sure you'd still be here.

Lizzie You think I've been waiting for you? I've got bombs to make, case you hadn't noticed.

Lucas What's in it? What's in your bomb?

Lizzie (*spits*) Paint, diesel oil, dirt, feathers. KFC bones. This is how I killed my dad. Dark voodoo. Oozy gunk from a gutter. Holy water. Bile, spit. Old-lady hair. Dead things. Violence.

Awkward pause . . .

So, now you're back . . .

Lucas And you're really pleased to see me . . .

Lizzie See those weeds, growing in the dirt? Pushing up. Through the dust. Those are very pissed-off weeds.

Lucas   You could put some in your bomb?

Lizzie   It's *my* bomb.

Lucas   Right, yeah . . . I get it! I shouldn't have come here. I just thought we'd do some catching up?

Lizzie   Did you now? Well, sorry, Lucas, but I'm late for work and then next Tuesday I'm definitely going to Bolivia. Yourself?

Lucas   Thought I'd go and see the old house.

Lizzie (*laughs ruefully*)   Lucas, you think the Futurist is in a bad state, your old house is a big hole in the ground.

She goes. He's left alone in the ruins and doesn't like it. He huddles up in his leather jacket as the dust falls down. A hallucination of the past is gathering around him, lighting up the shadows.

Scene Five
THE OWL

The past. Dusk.

*The boys are running wild through gutters, down alleys, carrying sticks and bricks and **Alan** is carrying an air rifle. They whoop and holler.*

Alan   Bloody hell, Lucas! It's here, down the alley!

*An owl flies ahead of them and, exhausted, is finally trapped down a blind alley. **Alan** points the gun at the owl.*

Alan   Blam! Blam! Dead owl, dead fucking owl!

He stops and looks in horror at the bird, turns and walks away. Game over. The owl is fluttering, frightened.

Spike   It's just . . . fluttering in the dust. It's not dead!

***Alan** pushes past them, really freaked.*

Lucas   WHERE ARE YOU GOING?

Alan   Game over. Can't do it. You go too far. I'm going cadging ciggies . . .

He is walking, breathing wildly, shocked by what they've done. Then suddenly . . .

Lucas   Finish the job.

Alan *stops and looks at him, shocked.*

Lucas   Finish the job off.

Alan   I don't want to . . .

Stephen   Leave him, Luke. He doesn't want to . . .

Spike   It's al lright. I'll do it if he doesn't want to.

Stephen   Maybe it'll be all right if we just walk away . . .

Spike   Nah. Give me the gun.

He goes to take the gun off **Alan***, who is still trying to walk away but* **Lucas** *is stopping him.*

Lucas   Give me the gun. (*Pause.*) Give . . . me . . . the gun.

He snatches the gun off **Alan***, turns it first on* **Spike** *then turns it on the owl and lets the bird have it. The bird falls, shuddering, and dies as they watch.*

Stephen   Ah, this is sick . . .

And then **Lucas** *picks the bird up by the scruff of its neck and walks towards the now weeping* **Alan***. He holds it up to* **Alan***'s face.* **Alan** *is revolted. He strains his neck to get away from the owl. But* **Lucas** *shoves it in his face.*

Spike   You shitting animal! I'm supposed to be the animal in this gang. I didn't think you'd really kill it. We'll be cursed . . .

He goes to confront **Lucas** *but* **Stephen** *gets in his way.*

Stephen   Get the fuck out of it! You're making things worse.

Lucas *looks at all of them, wild-eyed, holding the dead owl.* **Spike** *is in some kind of ecstatic heaven or hell.* **Alan** *is livid . . .*

Alan   This is my gang. You bastard. I let you in and now you've made this happen. And now we're cursed.

He is crying. **Lucas** *goes to him but* **Alan** *is too hurt to let him close.* **Lucas** *is breathing deeply, dead owl in hand. What he doesn't see is that* **Lizzie** *has arrived in the heat of this nightmare.*

Stephen   You are a mental case, Lucas.

Alan   When I'm dead, you'll be sorry . . .

It's as if the dark spirit of the dead owl is passing into **Alan** *as he speaks.* **Spike** *is shaking, pulling at his hair.* **Lizzie** *is watching, shocked by what she sees.*

Spike   What the hell's he on about? No one's gonna die . . .

Alan   Yes they are! Death's the big one. When I'm dead I don't want you here. You have to *go*. And never come back. Do you hear me? Lucas?

Lucas *is scared. He's shocked even himself. As he looks at* **Alan** *he kind of looks right through him – right into the eyes of* **Lizzie** *who is seeing the raw, ugly truth of this terrible event.* **Lucas** *and* **Lizzie** *lock into eye-contact. And then* **Lucas** *pushes on through them all, out of his mind with the death of a beast.*

Lucas   Right. OK . . . Yeah . . . Jesus . . . Yeah . . .

Trying to get his breath back, holding the dead owl, he hurries away.

Scene Six
BEDTIME STORY

The present. Friday evening.

Liverpool in all its madness. There is the cacophony of traffic, car horns, buses, taxis. A woman, **Val***, walks down the street.*

Val   Yeah, if you're looking for the Culture Company you go past the subway, turn left at Betfred, keep going till you get to Cash Converters and you come to a derelict church next to another Cash Converters. Cross over towards the pawnbrokers and then just keep going past the Viva Las Vegas amusement arcade, Posh Nails, the closed-down pub, Paddy Power, Sun Kissed Tanning Salon, Ladbrokes, Betfred, Subway, Coral, Betfred. Then you want to keep going for about a hundred yards towards Poundland . . .

And it's there between two Betfreds.

The woman walks away. **Lucas** *is waiting for* **Spike***, checking his phone. At the bus stop* **Elsie** *rocks back and forth. She's clearly troubled and her face is glistening with tears – even though she's laughing. She has a trolley full of rubbish, which she checks occasionally.*

Elsie   I've never been so happy in me life! I've never been so happy in me life! I've never been so bloody happy in me life!

Lucas *stops.*

Lucas   You OK, love?

Elsie   I've never been so happy in me life!

Lucas   I know you, don't I? Know you from long ago . . .

Elsie   Oh, everyone knows Elsie, love. I'll tell you this though . . .

She takes out a hankie and wipes away tears.

I have never been so bloody happy. In my life.

Lucas   That's good to hear. Can I get you anything?

Elsie   Can you get me Stewart Granger?

Lucas   I'll see what I can do?

Elsie   Or Charlton Heston when he was in *The Bible*?

Lucas   I'll have a good go. Long as you're all right?

Elsie   I've never been so happy in me life. I've never been so bloody happy in me life . . .

*She carries on insisting how happy she is as the tears roll down her face.
Perched on the edge of a rooftop there is a shadowy boy. This is*
Calumn, *fifteen, surrounded by birds, flying around him.*

Lucas   Look at that kid! Hey!

Calumn   What do you want, you dick?

Lucas   Come down. Come down before you fall.

Calumn   What do you care, arl-arse?

He climbs down. He stops by **Elsie** *and takes something out of his
pocket and gives it to her.*

Calumn   Here y'are, missus. Got you some lip-salve. Don't
want you getting chapped.

Elsie   Oh you lovely young boy!

She dips her fingers in the lip salve and rubs it over her lips as **Calumn**
goes to **Lucas***, who is taking out his tobacco.*

Calumn   You're new round here, aren't you?

Lucas   Not so new I'm bothered by a runt like you.

Calumn*'s got his earbuds in, 'tsk tsk tsk' leaking out. He holds out his
hand for a smoke.* **Lucas** *passes him the tobacco and, irritated by the
noise, he pulls* **Calumn***'s earbuds out.* **Calumn** *finds this funny and
nods at* **Lucas***'s cheek.*

Calumn   Not safe for an old man to be out you know.
She'll be fine but you won't last five minutes.

Lucas   You cheeky get.

Calumn   I'm only trying to look after you. There's kids on
stunt bikes razzing up and down this street. Dangerous street.
Dangerous kids.

Lucas   I can look after meself.

Calumn   Well, if you need the toilet or anything . . .

Lucas   I'm not that old . . .

Calumn   You're old enough to know better. Hanging round the street this time of night. Anything could happen.

Lucas   Like what?

Calumn   You could lose your bus pass. Believe me, mate, Lime Street's no place for an arl-arse like yourself . . .

Lucas   And what about you?

Calumn   Me? I'm a small trader. I've got this town sewn up in terms of *emergency supplies.*

Lucas   You're a dealer . . .

Calumn   Bit of this, bit of that. Nothing big. Top Trumps. Prescription drugs. Wotsits. Monster Munch. Weed. No cocaine though. Cocaine is immoral.

Lucas *acknowledges* **Calumn***'s moral standards.*

Calumn   Loyalty card! Gets the punters hooked. Wrote me own job description. Business plan. Risk assessment. All in place. Got the idea from Netmums.com.

Laughing, he puts his earbuds back in. 'Tsk, tsk, tsk . . . ' He gets on his bike and hands **Lucas** *a card.*

Calumn   Right, I'm off. If you need anything – beta blockers, mobility scooter – me number's on the card.

He heads off. As **Spike** *turns up he waves to* **Calumn***, who gives him the finger.* **Spike** *laughs and shakes his head like a fond uncle.*

Spike   Lovely kid!

Lucas   You know him?

Spike   Yeah. That's Lizzie's lad. Calumn. Credit to his mam.

Lucas *is stunned. He watches* **Calumn** *taking off on his stunt bike.* **Spike** *walks on ahead, laughing.*

Spike   So, how's your holiday going?

Lucas   I'm not on holiday, Spike. I've come home.

Spike   Ah right, yeah . . . have you got somewhere to stay then?

Lucas   Yeah, yeah . . . well not exactly, no . . .

Spike *stops outside the Futurist and takes his crowbar from inside his coat. He uses it to lift up the cinema's steel shutters. He holds the crowbar up to* **Lucas**.

Spike   Have to get yourself a door key then . . . I'm assuming you're staying the night?

Lucas   What, in here?

Spike   Yeah. I'm squatting. Sleep here? If you want to? It's freezing like, but I'll lend you a vest! Besides, I'm not that mad on being on me own. Stay. For the company?

Lucas   If it's not too much trouble . . .

Spike   No trouble. One or two plumbing horrors and it's not quite the Adelphi. Well, it's actually better than the Adelphi. So stay?

Lucas *smiles, nods and puts his rucksack down while* **Spike** *pokes around in the rubble and planks, gathering a sleeping bag and blankets and then disappearing into the shadows. As* **Lucas** *looks nervously around the cinema a ragged ghost, the seventeen-year-old* **Alan Icarus**, *emerges from the ruins and shadows. He whispers . . .*

Alan   What are you doing here, Lucas?

Lucas *takes out a cigarette and lights it.* **Alan** *flickers in the beams.*

Lucas   I thought I might watch an old film. (*It dawns on him.*) Jesus, Alan!

He moves towards **Alan** *but clouds of dust blow up and* **Alan** *scuttles away, feather and metal wings rattling as he goes.*

Shaken, **Lucas** *reaches out looking nervously around but there's no one there until* **Spike** *re-emerges from the dark recesses of the cinema carrying a bin bag. He sees* **Lucas**'s *fear.*

Spike   You all right mate?

Lucas   Hey? Yeah . . . I thought I saw something . . .
probably a bird . . .

Spike *hands him the bin bag.*

Spike   Open it . . .

Lucas *opens the bin bag and takes out his old crystal radio. He smiles.*

Lucas   My crystal radio! You kept it!

Spike   Tried to flog it down the car boot but no one was
arsed.

Lucas *sets the crystal set down in the dust and opens the box. A beam
of light bursts out.* **Lucas** *puts the headphones on. He adjusts the dial,
stretches out its wires.*

Lucas   Listen . . .

Whispering transmissions from ghost radio stations, static, voices . . .

Spike   There now, you're settling in already . . .

*He knocks some dust out of an old mattress and shakes out some blankets
on to the cast-iron bed. He lies down and nods to* **Lucas** *to get in.*

Spike   Best sleeping together otherwise we'll freeze and
wake up dead. And watch out for me nits . . .

Lucas *reluctantly climbs in. They wriggle around beneath the blankets.*

Lucas   And in our dreams we are airborne, slipping the
bonds of the earth, flying on a wing and a prayer over the
rooftops of Liverpool . . . or we would be if you'd keep
flaming still.

They struggle to sleep. **Spike** *sits up.*

Spike   A bedtime story'd help?

Lucas   Seriously?

Spike   Yeah, I sometimes tell meself one but one of yours'd
be boss!

Lucas   OK . . . OK . . . I remember . . . I remember when I was a kid, walking down the street, following some parade and this horse was coming towards me . . .

Spike   I was there. I was pissed.

Lucas   You were eight.

Spike   I was still pissed.

Lucas   Anyway, just as I'm about to reach up and touch the horse, it starts to kind of . . . fold up . . . its legs buckling beneath itself . . . And the horse man is pleading with it, pleading not to die . . .

Spike   Isn't this boss!

Lucas   And then it starts to bleed. At first it comes like spit, like it's been hit. But then it starts to pour out of its mouth and nose. Masses of the stuff just pumping out, dark brown and red and black. Gushing.

It was obscene . . . but it was beautiful as well.

Spike *is lost in childlike wonder, but also loving the horror of the scene.*

Spike   Blimey, Luke, a bleeding-to-death horse must be the most beautiful thing in the world . . .

Lucas   And then it was on the floor and it was twitching and shaking and this man was lying down next to it, holding it. He had his coat on it . . .

Spike *gets closer to* **Lucas***, almost cuddling in.*

Lucas   And then it kind of kicked as it raised its head and the last of the blood was seeping out and spreading around its head.

And then it was still.

And we stood there looking at it and the big massive crowd went as quiet as a prayer.

Pause. The horse is dead.

Lucas I was with my dad and I had hold of his hand and I looked at him and he was in tears. Well, and that got me going and we just stood there looking at a poor dead horse.

He sits there, remembering. **Spike** *is moved by the story. They can almost see the horse.* **Spike** *in a hushed awe says . . .*

Spike Make it come to life!

Lucas *takes his time, letting the tension and wonder build. And then . . .*

Lucas OK . . . So I walked up to it and touched it and I told it, 'Come on, don't be silly.' And it looked at me and struggled to its feet. And everybody gasped. And then it walked away and the horse man shook my hand and everybody clapped and sang 'For He's a Jolly Good Fellow!' And the horse was alive and the world was OK . . .

Spike *is moved and enchanted.*

Spike I fucking love that story.

It's like the resurrection of Jesus if Jesus was a horse!

As **Spike** *settles down, comforted by the memory of a poor dying horse,* **Lucas** *sits for a moment, remembering. A Lime Street woman –* **The City** *– sits on the steps of the Futurist and sings a beautiful lullaby.*

LULLABY

The City
    The day has gone and what has it left?
    Drift in the dark, drown in the world
    A sunset for the blind, a song for the deaf
    Drift in the dark, drown in the world
    But crystals of frost dress up the weeds
    Drift in the dark, drown in the world
    And teardrops ice into bracelets of beads
    Drift in the dark, drown in the world

    And the earth rolls round
    And all can be still now
    The scatter of slate

The arms of the cranes
And the last long sigh of the river's tide

As her voice filters through the shutters **Lucas** *lies down and the woman's lullaby soothes them both to sleep.*

Scene Seven
A MATTER OF LIFE AND DEATH

The past. Evening.

The cinema fire-exit door opens and the gang of kids – **Lucas**, **Alan Icarus**, **Stephen**, **Spike** *and* **Lizzie** *– come crawling in on their knees, along the front row as a film flickers above them. They sit cross-legged, gazing up at the screen as the opening music plays. They light cigarettes and smoke, blowing smoke rings.* **Lizzie** *loves the smoke.*

Lizzie   Ooh, I love a boy that smokes. I reckon the boys who can blow smoke rings are the ones who make best kissers. And the ones who make best kissers are the bad boys . . .

They like the sound of this. Apart from **Alan** *who is furious they all blow smoke like tiny chimneys.*

Lizzie   Oh you smoky boys! Will I do dip-dip-dip? Or will we play catch-a-girl, kiss-a-girl? Will I kiss you all or will I just choose a special boy as if it's bloody Christmas?

Spike   Kiss me if you want. Kiss me, Lizzie! Kiss me like you're the posh bird in the film!

Alan   I'll kill you if you kiss my sister.

Spike   Why?

Alan   Because she's my sister and I'm not having her kissing any of you.

Lizzie   I'll kiss who I want, Alan Icarus. I'll kiss Lucas if I'm bothered.

She goes to **Lucas** *and pulls him towards her mouth. He pulls away. She pulls him back. They kiss nervously at first and then longer, much to* **Alan**'s *dismay.*

s no one going to do anything about this bastard?

They shrug and avoid eye-contact.

Everyone does what Lucas wants! What happened to *my* gang?

They clam up. Only **Spike** *is brave enough or foolish enough to speak.*

Spike Lucas just has better ideas. Like going down the cut on a polystyrene raft or climbing the Dock Road chimney. It's all mad bastard stuff and he can kiss your sister.

Alan *looks to* **Stephen** *for support.* **Stephen** *shrugs.*

Stephen If he wants to kiss her. Yeah . . .

Alan *is bewildered. The film begins . . .*

Alan Fucking *hell*. It's starting. We doing this or what?

Spike Course we're doing it.

Alan Right, this bit's all stiff upper lip. Do it dead posh.

And then the muffled voices of A Matter of Life and Death *as David Niven in his plummeting, fireball aeroplane falls in love with radio operator June.*

Lucas *and* **Lizzie** *start acting it out with* **Alan** *interrupting now and then as he directs the scene. To* **Alan** *this really* is *a matter of life and death.*

Lizzie Request your position, request your position, come in Lancaster, come in Lancaster.

Lucas Position nil, repeat nil, age 27, 27. Did you get that? That's very important. What's your name?

Lizzie I cannot read you, cannot read you, request your position, come in Lancaster, come in Lancaster.

Lucas You seem like a nice girl, I can't give you my position, instruments gone, crew gone too, all except Bob here my sparks, he's dead.

Alan (*to* **Stephen**)   You can be Bob. Just be a dead fella . . .

Lucas   Inner port's on fire, I'm bailing out presently, I'm bailing out . . . Take a telegram.

Lizzie   Received your message, we can hear you, are you wounded? Repeat are you wounded? Are you bailing out?

Lucas   What's your name?

Lizzie   June.

Lucas   Yes, June, I'm bailing out, I'm bailing out but there's a catch, I've got no parachute.

Alan   Stop looking at each other, you're in two different places . . .

Lucas   Don't be afraid, June, we've had it and I'd rather jump than fry. After the first thousand feet I shan't know anything anyway. I say, I hope I haven't frightened you.

Lizzie   No, I'm not frightened.

Lucas   Good girl. June? Are you pretty?

Lizzie   Not bad, I . . .

Lucas *goes a bit Scouse, which irritates* **Alan**.

Lucas   You've gorra good voice, you've got guts too . . .

Alan   Shitting hell! Do the posh voice!

Lucas   It's funny, I've known dozens of girls, I've been in love with some of them, but it's a girl whom I've never seen and never shall see who'll hear my last words, it's rather sweet. June, if you're around when they pick me up, turn your head away.

Lizzie   I could love a man like you, Peter.

Oh, come on Alan, I feel stupid saying that . . .

Alan   Just say the bloody lines!

Lucas   I love you June, you're life and I'm leaving you. I was lucky to get you, June. Can't be helped about the parachute, I'll have my wings soon anyway, big white ones. What do you think the next world's like? I've got my own ideas . . .

Lizzie   Oh, Peter . . .

Lizzie *and* **Lucas** *reach out and hold hands.*

Alan   What you doing? You can't hold his hand! He's in a burning aeroplane, you dick!

Lucas   I'll know soon enough anyway. I'm signing off now, June, goodbye, goodbye June . . .

Lizzie   Hello G for George, hello G George, hello G George, hello . . .

Lucas   Goodbye . . . goodbye . . .

Lucas *acting out being in a burning bomber, falling from the sky,* **Spike** *and* **Stephen** *exploding like bombs.*

Stephen   G for George! G for George!

Spike   That was boss!

They leap up laughing with delight giving V signs to the cinema audience and usherettes, punching the air, swaggering out loudly, still exploding like bombs, **Alan** *in the middle of them laughing at the chaos they have caused.*

Scene Eight
VOODOO

The present. Saturday morning.

A woman – **Audrey** *– stops.*

Audrey   'Old woman whose clothes are old and the eyes of whose heart are darkened, seek out the spiritual fountain of the city and lift the eyes of your mind to the ghost of Arthur Dooley and then you will renew your youthful rebellious spirit and soar like the eagle . . . ' is what I wanted to have tattooed on me backside but it was too much to fit in . . .

So I got a map of Liverpool – drawn to scale – done on me left bicep and tricep. And on various parts of me torso I got an entire menagerie of chameleon, armadillo, salamander, basilisk and various ornithologicals such as nightingale and raven . . . and what I am is Lime Street Zoo . . . a zoo on two legs tattooed lady and do you want to see? Do you want to see?

Well, you'll have to take my word for it cos I'm not getting my tats out for no one . . .

She walks away. In the cinema **Lizzie** *is uncoiling cables.* **Lucas** *and* **Spike** *are half asleep, tussling for the blankets, finally giving up and getting out of bed.* **Spike** *is stretching and scratching.*

Spike   Morning, Lizzie love. You know what, that was the tenderest love making I have ever experienced.

Lucas   Piss off, Spike!

Lizzie   I've told you before about taking in strays.

Spike *gets up and starts interfering, getting in* **Lizzie**'s *way.*

Spike   Need any help, Lizzie love?

Lizzie   No, I don't. Get out from under me feet . . .

Spike (*to* **Lucas**)   She's a dab hand with a screwdriver, our Lizzie . . .

Lucas   We could help you? If we knew what you were doing.

Lizzie   The pair of you, just leave me alone. I'm busy.

Spike   She's up to something. Something to do with them wires . . . Am I right, Liz? Is it something to do with them wires?

Lizzie   Course it's something to do with the shitting wires! Jesus tonight . . .

She slams down her tools as **Stephen** *comes in carrying a box full of fabric and armfuls of clothes in dry-cleaner bags. He's distressed.*

Lizzie   Oh here we go, fuck-up number three . . .

He drops his stuff and slumps. He looks hurt.

Lizzie   I'm only joking, Ste. What happened to you?

Stephen   Got kicked out me flat. Had a few to drink after
the Open Mic at Greasy Pete's. Go home, don't know why
but I have a little dance. In the kitchen finishing off the
Christmas sherry and when I have a dance I like to sing.

Lizzie   What do you sing?

Stephen   Not songs. Women's names. Not like me Auntie
Vera or your mam. I'm not saying nothing about your mam,
but not like your mam . . . Anyway, someone phones the
landlord, says there's a nutter singing. Next thing the landlord's
banging on the door, lets himself in with his master key. Next
thing you know the landlord's locked in the airing cupboard.

Spike   You've got a lock on your airing cupboard?

Stephen   Yes. And I'm thinking, I'll keep him in there. Not
for ever. One week, maybe two but he's on his mobile saying,
'I'm being held hostage by a man wearing Laura Ashley.'
And it's not Laura Ashley, it's vintage. And then it's the
police and then I'm bin-bagged in the gutter. Just for singing
women's names.

Spike   What women, Ste? Sing them to us . . .

Stephen   It's more like a sort of litany . . .

Spike   In your own way, Ste. As it suits you . . .

Stephen *breathes deeply, exhales and starts to sing. As he does so,*
Lucas *draws near, listening to* **Stephen***'s beautiful list of names.*

Stephen
    Candy Darling
    Kim Novak
    Edie Sedgwick

    Sinead . . . O wild Sinead . . .

Stephen *stops, shyly.* **Spike** *encourages him to sing into it.*

Spike   Tender and sweetly, Ste, as you were . . .

Stephen
Nico
Lana Turner
Patsy Cline
Juliette Greco
Maria Callas
Jane Birkin
Judy Garland

Diana Dors

Diana fucking Dors!

Spike, **Lizzie** *and* **Lucas** *are moved by the strange, sweet song.*

Spike   Only Ste could come up with that . . .

Stephen   I sing their lovely names. I want to take them home with me and let them colour in my dreams. But now I can't because I've got no home.

Spike *smiles gently, nods at his friend as they contemplate the sadness and beauty of it all. And then . . .*

Spike   Well, you can live here as long as you stop that bleedin' awful singing.

Stephen   That's just . . . mean.

Lizzie   He's joking.

Spike   Come and freeze to death with us in the Palace of Dreams.

Stephen   I'll write a song about it . . .

Spike   Yeah. Do that. I'll make you a bed of old tyres and hubcaps and you can write a lovely song . . .

Spike *stands up and gives* **Stephen** *a hug.*

Spike   Right. Now let's get your box of frocks and get you settled in.

Spike *and* **Lucas** *pick up* **Stephen***'s stuff and carry it to the bed.
As* **Lizzie** *gets back to work with the wires,* **Stephen** *is drawn to the
tangles of old film. He drapes lengths of old film around his shoulders and
parades before them in all his glory.*

Stephen   Hey! Look at me. I'm wearing the history of
cinema! Hitchcock blondes and Disney girls . . .

Spike   The boy's a genius!

Stephen   Like a coat made of kisses and gunslingers' spurs.

*He dances gently, the coat of old film stock rustling as he falls into a
reverie of wonder.*

I am the prince of arousal and desire! Of chaos, wild children
and whip-crack-away!

Lucas *takes the cable* **Lizzie***'s been working on. She takes it back.*

Lucas   I've been thinking . . .

Lizzie   That's all we bloody need.

Lucas   I reckon we could wire the rooftops up for broadcast,
spin a few voices out across the night. Turn the buildings into
massive speaker cabinets.

Spike   Pirate radio!

Lucas   Yeah, imagine walking down Church Street and
you heard Spike, telling the world about the apocalypse, or
Ste's lovesongs to the city . . .

Stephen   Like the Morse code of the heart . . .

Lucas   Filtering into the council chambers! A little bit of
mischief. What do you think, Lizzie?

Lizzie *is stretching out cables, screwdriver in hand.*

Spike   Yeah, Lizzie, what do you think?

Lizzie   Me? I'm not that arsed right now about Lucas and
his ideas. I'm trying to get stuff sorted for you, Spike, and
you lot just keep pissing about. And now Lucas appears to

be living here too. Why are you here? I mean, why come back? Now.

An uncomfortable pause.

Lucas   I just wanted to come home . . .

He's got the cables again. Really annoying her.

Lizzie   You're still playing games.

Lucas   Remember the cinema and bonfire night and the dirty old canal? Do you not still live in magical places, Lizzie?

She seizes the cables and connects them. It's like she's switching on the universe. ZAP!

Instantly with a whoosh the cinema is bathed in glowing light, an illuminated grotto. They gaze upon its wonders.

Lizzie   Magical places? How's that for fucking magic!

*Motes of dust dance in luminous beauty. The gang bathe in it. The Futurist is a vision of splendour. They are stunned, enchanted by its beauty, but **Lizzie** is gathering her things.*

Lizzie   Part-time access course. 'Electrical Beginners'. Cos I live in a practical world too. Right, I'm out of here. Enjoy your electricity.

Lucas   Where you going?

Lizzie   I'm off to invoke a curse on a malign institution using a hex adapted from voodoo sorcerers.

Lucas *doesn't know what the hell to make of this. She's glad. She carries on.*

Lizzie   Yeah . . . What you do is, you seal an old Lucozade bottle with black wax and inside there's . . . graveyard dirt and a curse spelled out in, like . . . toenail clippings and the sweat of crushed ambition and desire . . .

Lucas   What?

Lizzie   Yeah. I'm striding into the Town Hall. With me voodoo curse.

Lucas   Jesus . . .

Lizzie   But first of all I'm taking my Calumn to the dentist. Oh yeah, if any of them bastards from the lap-dancing club come asking why we're stealing their power? Tell 'em it's a tax on their council-licensed, squalid bloody morals.

They all watch her go. **Lucas** *is shell-shocked,* **Stephen** *admiring,* **Spike** *laughing with delight.*

Spike   Off she goes with a bee in her brain! Isn't she boss with her toenail bomb?

He turns to the others.

When we kick off with the radio, you gonna sing some tunes, Ste?

Stephen   I might do. If I do, I might sing something French.

He whisper-sings, taking the piss a bit, his voice echoing around the building.

Les sanglots longs
Des violons
De l'automne
Blessent mon coeur
D'une langueur
Monotone . . .

Spike   I reckon that's definitely French! What does it mean?

Stephen   No idea. Saw it in a war film. Some kind of signal . . .

Lucas   French Resistance radio! It means the uprising is about to begin . . .

Spike *wants a turn. He grabs a box and climbs on to it.*

Spike   I'm gonna stand on this box when I'm on the radio.

Lucas   No one listening'll know you're standing on it though, Spike . . .

Spike   If Ste can wear a frock, I can stand on a box.

He does so. He speaks in a voice of doom . . .

The scar has split wide open and everything is coming to the surface. Centipedes and slithering things, oozing through the cracks.

Stephen *is taking the piss, teasing him.*

Stephen   It's not just insects running wild. I saw a leopard in Poundland!

Spike   Is right! I'm telling you, Lucas, this city is *alive.*

Lucas   But they hope we haven't noticed . . .

Spike (*knowledgeable*)   They're scared. And that's why they have their teeth whitened.

Stephen   Big bloody leopard by the Brillo Pads and bleach . . . I'm telling you. In *Poundland.*

Spike   Serious. Them grinning liars on the telly. Dazzling gnashers. The Mayor . . .

Stephen   Well, maybe not the Mayor . . .

Spike   It's like their shiny teeth are shields against the horror . . .

Stephen   Big massive leopard asking the shelf-stacker – 'Can you recommend anything to get rid of this rash?'

He takes hold of **Lucas**'s *mouth and examines his teeth.*

Spike   You've got really honest gums, Lucas, but I can't tell if you're an honest man or a liar.

Stephen   No change there then!

Spike   Hey! Be nice. (*To* **Lucas**.) Go on, Luke. Do some radio stuff.

Lucas *stands on the soapbox and as he speaks his voice echoes through the building.*

Lucas   Resist and rise up! Rise up against the philistine forces! This is the voice of Free Liverpool, calling out to the nighthawks, coming live to you from the city's beating heart . . .

His voice echoes through the cinema, out into the city and across its rooftops. And then the sound of car horns, taxi horns, bus horns comes in from the streets. They look at each other, smiling.

And then a seismic shudder comes. Pieces of the building fall. Dust drops. Beneath their feet – as if they are in an earthquake zone – the ground begins to rupture. A crack appears . . . **Spike** *is ecstatic.*

Scene Nine
ALAN'S GHOST

The flicker of ghosts. **Lucas** *sets the crystal radio down and unravels the wires, stretching them across the rooftop. And again: voices, echoes, distortion, wind in the wires.* **Lucas** *sees* **Alan**'s *ghost, wearing his flying goggles and feather and metal wings.* **Alan** *is flying in his mind, transformed into a bird.*

Alan
   The whistling of the wind.
   I fly through the tornado.
   My aeroplane is shaking.
   The earth is a blurred curve.
   I have no power over the weather.
   I am in the hands of . . . an angel.
   But the angel lets me . . . fall.

   I hold on to the horizon with one hand.
   I hold on to the controls with the other.
   My plane is disintegrating and I am . . .
   Falling . . .

Across the vast eternity I am flying,
falling upwards to the stars . . .

Spike   It's coming! The city's wound is opening.

He looks at **Stephen***, who is holding himself tight as if to keep himself safe. Then* **Spike** *looks wild-eyed at* **Lucas***, who is looking at the ground in awe and fear. They look at each other.* **Spike***'s apocalyptic vision is coming true. Light spills from the wound as music plays.*

Alan *appears to fall. Upwards. He turns and looks down to* **Lucas***. He folds his wings around himself.*

Alan   Penny for your thoughts, Lucas?

Lucas   I was thinking, long way down and what would it feel like . . .

Alan   It feels amazing! I nearly touched the sun. I had golden wings. I never jumped. I flew. With great conviction. But as I swooped and soared, my wax melted. I fell through vapour trails, fell through the blue . . . I walked the edge of possibility. You win some, you lose some. Oh fuck! Falling, falling for ever . . . Come and join me. Fly. Walk off the roof and fly . . .

Lucas   I can't. I don't want to . . .

Alan *descends to the street. He walks along* **Spike***'s mythical crack in the earth, which is volatile now, unstable. He touches the ground and it moves beneath his fingers.*

Alan   It's easy. You just have to lick the battery. If you wanna fly.

He points out across the city at the turbulent sky – as turbulent as the ground beneath his feet.

Alan   You're scared, aren't you, Lucas?

Lucas   Yeah. I'm scared of being here. With you . . .

Alan   You're scared of living. Of really living . . .

Lucas   I'm scared of you.

Alan   Just step into the sky. Step over the edge. You have to be able to step with grace across the shining edge . . .

Lucas *looks over the shining edge. And the pavements of Lime Street are buckling like a rupturing. The ground is ripped, is rent asunder. The crack in the guts of Liverpool is agony for the city and for the people and creatures in it. And* **Alan** *steps lightly along the length of the crack as the light spills out.*

Scene Ten
THE DIRTY OLD CANAL

The past. A summer's afternoon.

The gang – seventeen and eighteen years old – is down by the canal, messing about on the towpath. **Alan Icarus** *is wearing a shirt and loose tie. He's fishing with a home-made rod and* **Spike** *is lying down on his belly, scooping a jam jar into the water. They're drinking beer from cans, passing round a spliff.* **Stephen** *is peering into the water.* **Lizzie** *is sunbathing.* **Lucas** *walks up the towpath and joins them.*

Stephen   Thank God school is over.

Lizzie   Yeah, but me dad the bastard was on about us getting jobs . . .

Stephen   There are no jobs. Don't want one anyway . . . (*He draws on the spliff.*) I just want to over-indulge in top-grade weed . . .

Lucas   Alan got the last job in Liverpool!

Alan   Yeah. And I didn't even want one. Went in pissed. No one noticed.

Stephen   Should have worn your wings.

Alan   I did wear me wings. They didn't even interview me. 'How soon can you start?' I said I can't start cos I have to fly a mission over occupied France. Didn't turn a hair.

Stephen   Should have worn your glue-on moustache . . .

Alan   I did wear me glue-on moustache. Full-on handlebar.
No one bloody noticed. They said I was highly qualified.
I told 'em I never had any quals. They said it didn't matter,
I was still more qualified than any of the others. Any man
who flies missions over occupied France is *in*. Stupid job.
Filing clerk. Fucking stupid job. It's not even a proper job.

Lucas   There are no proper jobs . . .

Alan (*sucking deep on the spliff*)   I mean, it's a proper job that's
not a proper job . . .

Lizzie   Right, well we know what Alan's thinking . . .
What's Stephen thinking?

Stephen   Hey? Ah, I was thinking about glam rock. You
could be built like a brick shit-house but you could still wear a
dress. I was sitting here thinking – what this canal needs is a
touch of feather boa . . .

Spike   Are you still going through a phase?

Stephen   No, I'm just dreaming of the glam rock revival.
Right here on the canal. We're in this band, right? We get on
a ship and we sail down the canal. I'm the singer – wearing
pink – gorgeous rock star sailing down the cut. Waving at
screaming teenagers. And not drinking shit lager like this stuff.
No. Something cheeky – with a cork. And I'm singing . . .
(*Sings.*) 'A tangle of nylon, a cracked leather swag . . . ' Sailing
through my purple satin dreams. All the way to fucking
Leeds!

They're all looking at him. Transfixed.

Stephen   Well, you did ask.

Spike   OK. I was thinking, there's always one shoe. A
floating shoe. What happened to the other shoe? Who comes
down the canal and throws away one shoe?

Lizzie   I'd love to see one of them tropical fish. People let
them go. Why would you throw your angel fish in the dirty
old canal?

Lucas   One time I saw this pike, when I was a kid. Like a six-foot-long torpedo. They drained the water out and it was dying in the mud with all the prams. Wrapped around an old shopping trolley, gasping for breath. I had it in me hands and it was dying . . .

Lizzie   Everything dies in your stories!

Spike   You're sounding like a girl, Liz!

Lizzie   That's because I am a girl, you stupid get, as if you hadn't noticed.

Lucas *is crouching next to* **Lizzie**. *They smile at each other.*

Spike   Lucas has noticed. Lucas can't take his eyes off you.

Alan   Shut it. Lay a finger on her and I'll fucking kill you.

Lucas   Don't tell me who I can or cannot touch.

Lizzie   Stop talking about me as if I'm the bloody pike!

Lucas   Since when does a loser office boy get to give the orders? I mean, what a nothing job. Icarus the filing clerk!

Alan   You know what? Every day is like me death day, every day is driving me round the twist. But I've still got me dreams in here and I'm still Alan Icarus *in here.*

He taps his skull. Suddenly . . .

Oh shit!

And he starts reeling in his line.

Shitting hell! I reckon I've got one . . .

He can't handle whatever's on the end of the line. He's losing control.

Lucas   Give it here, you useless fuck . . .

He takes over, yanks the line in roughly. The line comes curling through the air. The pike has escaped the hook.

Alan   You've lost the fucker!

Spike   Pair of useless bastards!

Lucas   Fuck off, Alan, fuck off, Spike!

The hook spins towards **Spike**. *It catches his eyeball.*

And **Lucas** *yanks on the rod, pulling the line taut. He doesn't know the hook is caught . . .*

And then horrifically, **Spike** *is on the floor screaming as his eye is plucked out by the hook.*

Lizzie   Oh no, Spike! Spike!

Spike   Jesus shit. Oh Jesus shit!

An eye on a length of fishing line, spinning through the air.

As **Spike** *staggers, howling, there comes an apocalyptic scream, echoing down the dirty old canal, echoing through the years.*

Scene Eleven
THE KIDS'LL BE OK . . .

The present. Sunday morning.

A drunk – **Pete the Piss** *– staggers past, concerned about his wayward limbs.*

Pete   I can't get me leg going proper. It's doing that jerky twitch it does when I've had too many sherbets. Look at me leg! It's limbering up for the hokey cokey but it's not quite falling into place.

He points at his leg and studies it, swaying with the booze. It jerks.

It's not supposed to do that . . . It's not what's required . . . of a leg . . . Anyway, hokey cokey's shit on your own. You need at least ten people for a proper Hokey Cokey . . . and then there's the fucking conga . . . (*He sings.*) 'Aya aya CONGA, Aya aya CONGA ta na na na . . . ' (*Gives up.*) Well, what's the use in that? Hey? Anybody? What's wrong with youz? I'm desperate for a conga . . . Please your fucking selves . . . On top of everything I've gone and lost me kebab . . . Who's

stolen me kebab? Chicken tikka kebab on a bap with a dab of
Romesco . . . I'll kill that fucking seagull . . .

He staggers away. **Calumn** *burns rubber on his stunt bike, coming to a
halt right in front of* **Lucas**. **Lizzie** *is approaching. She stops some
distance away and watches with interest.* **Lucas** *is taking out his tobacco
and a lump of cannabis.*

Calumn   All right, arl-arse?

Lucas   Ah, the Boy Wonder. How's the world?

Calumn   You know what, right now while I'm wasting my
time talking to you, there are thousands of businessmen doing
back-hand deals in this city. Right now. Here in Brand
Liverpool. Carving it up between themselves and getting it
all wrong. But meanwhile, where the action is, young
entrepreneurs like me are actively driving the economy. Do
you think they've even noticed? They haven't got a clue . . .

*He holds his hand out for the tobacco and cannabis, takes it and begins
expertly rolling a one-skin spliff. He looks with distaste at* **Lucas**'s
cannabis.

Calumn   Where d'you buy this shit? You're smoking
contaminated weed, mate, that's your problem. That's why
your mind's fracked. Here, get on this . . .

He takes out a small bag of cannabis and waves it in front of **Lucas**'s
nose.

Lucas   What's in it?

Calumn *carries on building the spliff.*

Calumn   Ethically sourced cannabis. No pit-bull poo or
insecticide in that mate. Say what you like about the
government but they know how to grow top weed.

Lucas   Shouldn't you be in school? Then again, you don't
need school, do you?

Calumn   Nah. It's not for me. Forged a note to teacher off
me mam saying I was too mentally advanced for the curriculum

on offer. I'm sub-contracting anyway and – as is apparent –
education doesn't happen in the classroom, it happens on the
streets.

He passes **Lucas** *the spliff.* **Lucas** *eyes it suspiciously, then smokes,
wheezes, nods approvingly, takes the bag off* **Calumn** *and sticks it in
his jeans.*

Lucas   In Amsterdam . . .

Calumn   Oh here we go. (*Old man's voice.*) 'When I were a
lad we smoked umpteen Mary Janes afore breakfast . . . '
Now give me back me lucky bag.

Lucas   I'll look after it for you. I'm giving up. (*Smokes.*)
Tomorrow. When I've finished this!

Calumn   You're too old for drugs. Old and mental. Any
ADHD in your medical history? Or any other neurological
diseases?

Lucas   What *are* you on about?

Calumn   Come on, look at the state of you. I'm just trying
to get to the bottom of why you're such a fuck-up at your age.

Lucas   Sometimes I ask meself that question . . .

Calumn   Maybe your alcohol abuse is inhibiting your
glutamine. I can get you some amitrip . . .

Lucas *shakes his head, exasperated with this expert on mental disorder.*

Lucas   So, your mam . . . ? You know I've known her since
we were kids?

Calumn   Ha! We were talking about you last night. Reading
between the lines she's not exactly buying in to you and your
homecoming hero shit is she?

Lucas   I didn't come back for her . . .

Calumn   Yes you did. You're all the same, you geriatrics.
It's all dogs with two dicks when you get to your age.

He starts to go.

Now give me back me gear or cough up.

Lucas *takes out a crumpled fiver and gives it to him.*

Lucas   There. 1980s prices. What would your mam think?

Calumn   She never needs to know. So don't have any ideas. Right, loser, I've got a conference call . . .

He takes out his phone as he climbs on to his stunt bike.

Calumn   Word of advice?

Lucas   Go on . . .

Calumn   Fella your age, still wearing a leather jacket like that? It's, well, it's *unseemly* . . .

Lucas *has never felt so uncool. He nods, takes off the jacket and gives it to* **Calumn** *who puts it on, does some James Dean moves.*

Calumn   Let me know if you want any antipsychotics. Medical trials show modest benefits.

Lucas   For what?

Calumn   Dementia . . . impotence . . .

And away he speeds. **Lucas** *climbs up on to the rooftop and starts working away securing a radio transmitter.* **Lizzie** *arrives and climbs up to the roof lugging more gear tied up in a bundle. She drops it on the rooftop.*

Lizzie   Just heard on the radio – police in Liverpool have carried out a controlled explosion outside the Town Hall after potentially volatile substances were found in a purple wheelie bin. A woman in her forties with a long list of grudges is being sought for questioning.

Lucas   You didn't?

Lizzie   That'd be telling . . . So anyway, I think your pirate radio idea's all right.

Lucas   Overboard with the praise . . .

Lizzie   And I see you gave my Calumn your skanky leather jacket?

Lucas   Yeah, he thought it was dead cool.

Lizzie   Course he did. You and him have palled up then?

Lucas   Ah! Yeah, we were chatting about the school curriculum.

Lizzie   Course you were . . .

Still working away . . .

Lucas   He's like a cross between Pablo Escobar and Citizens Advice.

Lizzie   He's heading for trouble.

Lucas   Heading? He *is* the trouble.

Lizzie   Social Services on the doorstep all the time. He's worse than we were.

Lucas   It's just kids . . .

Lizzie   He is. He's worse. I had all these ideas about freedom. Went a bit earth mother. Let the boy roam. Everyone these days keeps their children under lock and key. My lad's gonna be out in the fields, I said. My lad's gonna be building tree houses. Running wild, out on his bike.

Lucas   He's out on his bike all right . . .

Lizzie   Sometimes I think I've lost him. He goes his own way . . .

Testing equipment, pulling switches.

Lucas   Takes after his mother. When you were a kid you were going to be a freedom-fighter in Bolivia.

Lizzie   Yeah. Well, exactly . . . and now I want to be a freedom-fighter here. I walk to the community action centre where I work – yeah, work, Lucas – and kids like my Calumn are there on the corners. Doing their deals. Tiny gangsters. What's going to happen to him and the others? Cos nobody

gives a fuck. What did we learn from our own wild childhoods?
They're the wild kids now and Jesus help them . . .

Anyway, I love my Calumn. He makes me laugh. He's a good
kid. I mean, he's a bad kid but he's a good kid underneath.

She looks at him looking at her, biting her lip . . .

He's a good kid so don't say a word against him. Anyone.

They've connected everything up.

Lizzie   This is it then. Radio Free Liverpool. Test
transmission! What'll it be?

Lucas   Let's broadcast Lime Street. The voices of the
night . . .

Lizzie *lowers a microphone down on its cable until it's hanging just
above* **Elsie** *down below in the street, talking to herself. They look down
at her.*

Elsie   When I was young I smelled of lilac and the boys
wanted to kiss me, so they kissed me. As boys do. We'd have
a cuddle in the snug and a kiss in the saloon. And then we'd
have electric in our bellies down the bloody alley, and all the
boys were mad for me, they loved my pretty skin. But one day
I looked in my compact mirror as I brushed my hair and my
curls were white, and I was an old woman, wasn't pretty any
more. I had turned white as winter . . .

And pretty Elsie had disappeared while I wasn't looking. I
was lonely so I'd talk to myself, sit in bus stops beneath my
umbrella. Singing and whispering, like the other mad old
ducks. Then one day I was sitting in the bus shelter and a
young girl came by and asked me for a hug.

Lucas *hits a button. The transmitter works. They capture the sounds of
Lime Street – voices echoing, singers, car horns, birds – as* **Elsie** *speaks
to herself.* **Elsie***'s reverie goes 'live'. It's beautiful.* **Lizzie** *and* **Lucas**
glance at each other.

Elsie   And so we hugged and, oh! she smelled of lilac and
I held her so tight I could have stolen her bones. Then, when

I watched her walk away, I realised she was me. She was me when I was young and pretty in the days when all the boys wanted to kiss me. And I realised I am lucky because I have been loved . . . The children will be OK if we let them, if we help them. The children will be OK if we love them one and all.

She waves at shadows and dances away. **Lucas** *and* **Lizzie** *watch her go. They look at each other. Something special has happened. There is a moment between them of something shared . . . and then* **Lizzie** *breaks it.*

Lizzie   It works! We're on the air. We start tonight.

She climbs down off the rooftop, leaving **Lucas** *up there, hanging over the edge, microphone dangling like a fishing line catching the sounds of the night.*

Scene Twelve
DEAD CROW

The past. Dusk.

Teenage **Lucas** *walks down the canal towpath carrying a dead crow. He finds* **Lizzie***, lying on a raft made from old planks, oil drums and polystyrene. She slugs a bottle of light ale. She's surprised to see him. Nervous.*

Lizzie   You frightened me.

Lucas   What you doing here? We were all worried.

Lizzie   My dad's a bastard. Said I smelled of fags. I'm sevenfuckingteen. He said I'm grounded, I said fuck off, I ran away. I'm not going back. I slept on the fridge mountain but it stank so I came down here.

Lucas   We'll run away together. Just need some money then we'll run away. I'm going to Paris and you can come with me.

Lizzie   I'll spit in the ditch and wish me dad dead.

She spits. **Lucas** *spits. Laughter.*

Lucas   I've got something for you, Lizzie.

She looks at the dead bird in his hands.

Lizzie   You bring a girl a dead crow? You know how to treat 'em don't you?

Lucas   It's not the crow, it's what's inside the crow that matters.

He cuts into the dead bird and takes a heart-shaped locket out of its belly. He lets the dead crow fall to the ground.

Then he sticks his penknife into the mud of the towpath.

Turns out crows have golden hearts.

He dangles the locket, holds it out towards her. She reaches out to touch it.

Lizzie   Tomorrow it's my birthday. Is this my birthday present, Lucas? A dead bird's golden heart?

Lucas   Yes . . .

She takes the heart.

I want you to wear it. I want to put it round your neck and the pair of us to walk into every pub in town. Together.

He goes to her, takes a shoelace out of his boot and threads the lace through the locket. Then he goes behind her. He touches her neck gently and then ties the locket around her neck. He spins her around and looks at her.

You take my breath away, Lizzie, and now we're kind of married.

Lizzie   I'll never take it off.

Lucas   I'll marry you. Look after you. Take care of you. For ever. I just look at you . . . and want to . . . *touch* you . . .

Lizzie   Let's make sure no more bad things happen.

They kiss. The raft starts floating away, taking them 'downriver', down the canal.

Lucas   We're escaping. The harvest moon is shining. There are wild creatures in the reeds. The spider webs are dripping with golden honey. The owl is calling. The hunter is looking for us but he'll never find us. The moon is like God's eye. The river rolls . . .

They are watched by **Alan Icarus**, *who sneaks up and takes* **Lucas**'*s penknife out of the ground, holds it up so that it glints in the street light glare.*

Lucas   You've got flower seeds in your hair.

Lizzie   Maybe they'll grow and I'll have a hair-do full of cornflowers, buttercups and daisies.

Lucas   You're beautiful already. I don't think I could cope if your hair was full of flowers . . .

Lizzie   Run away for ever. That's what we'll do. We'll run away for ever till we die.

As **Alan** *walks away into the shadows,* **Lucas** *and* **Lizzie** *kiss. Tenderly at first, becoming more intense until they start to make love.* **The City** *sings and the others join in with the chorus.*

THE HOUR THE DAY MEETS THE DARK

The City
    It's the hour the day meets the dark
    When you don't know which path you should choose
    You can lie down and die with the sun
    Or you can rise with the moon

    The wind mutters yes yes yes
    The road knows the beat of your boot
    You've punched out the factory clock
    Brushed the moths from your suit

    And dance with us night-wolves, there's howls in our veins
    We're the match, we're the fuse, we're the flame
    In the night from the stars and the graves we are born
    But we go with the dawn

In the morning your head will pound hard
And all of the nightmares will wake
The morning will clang like a knell
But all that can wait

And dance with us now you've got howls in your veins
You're the match you're the fuse you're the flame
In the night from the stars and from the graves you are born
But you go with the dawn

As **Lucas** *and* **Lizzie** *drift towards the light of the silver moon.*

Scene Thirteen
FIRST BROADCAST

The present. Sunday evening.

Inside the cinema **Lucas** *is setting up for broadcast. It's like a squatted Broadcasting House in there.* **Stephen** *is at the piano, running through a melody. He hums along. Dust is falling.*

Stephen   Oh, listen to the moon crooner, singing songs where dust falls from the stars . . .

Spike *comes in with bursting carrier bags. He empties the bags, calls out.*

Spike   Get a load of this! Got these from a boarded-up library. I reckon we could have a library of our own!

Dozens and dozens of old books come tumbling out and he starts rummaging through them. He picks up a book and gives it to **Lizzie**.

Lizzie (*reads*)
    'That is no country for old men.
    The young in one another's arms, birds in the trees –
    Those dying generations – at their song,
    The salmon falls, the mackerel-crowded seas . . . '

Spike *nods approvingly.*

Spike   Fucking beautiful . . . it was like a poem.

Lucas   It *is* a poem. You should read it.

Spike   Still can't read, can I?

Lizzie   Then you should learn.

Spike   Too hard.

Lizzie   Come here, I'll show you.

She picks up a can of car paint and shakes it. Then she sprays on the wall.

HOW –

Lizzie   H ... O ... W.

Spike   'How'?

Lizzie   Yep ...

She sprays another word.

CAN –

Spike   I know that one. It's 'can'.

Lizzie   Here, copy that.

HOW CAN A BIRD THAT IS BORN FOR JOY ...

Spike *take the book and begins to write.*

Lucas *takes the microphone.*

Lizzie   Welcome to Radio Free Liverpool. This is our first broadcast. Wherever you're listening, on the car radio, in the bath, or even up on the rooftops ... as we go live across the city, this song is for you ...

*And **Lucas** delivers a spontaneous song. A kind of half-sung poem as **Stephen** and the musicians play.*

LIME STREET

Lucas
    Swimming in the guts of Bacchus
    Does this street have just one name?
    The only dread is that of silence

All the tongues discard their shame
But only here will you find the truth
Only here with the soothes
Of Lime Street

Dionysus came here once
Bought one drink, said that's enough for me
I've been some wild old joints
Left some money behind some bars
Soaked the walls with whisky brine
Soused the streets with sacred wine
But never have I been the first one home
To leave the fun on Lime Street

Though through the hours before the night
All are trodden, ground
Pissed on, shit on, chained up, worked up
Slaves to every pound
They earn or find or beg or steal,
We're all attached to a broken wheel,
But some are rolling in the grooves,
The ones that have no more to lose
The lights, the reels, the ragged seams
The polka reds, the neon green
The black-eyed nighthawks grind and growl
And dance, dance, amongst the howl
Of Lime Street

So when I've smoked this pinch of dust
And when I've sucked the last bone bare
When I've started eating rust
When the gulls have took my hair
I hope my bones will know to move
To drag me through this mud of men
To let me die amongst the gruel
The glorious gruel
Behind the moon
On Lime Street

Lizzie *is watching closely. Seeing him for the moment in a different light. When* **Lucas** *has finished,* **Lizzie** *goes to him. She kisses him lightly, quickly on the cheek. For a moment she looks at him sadly. He looks back at her.* **Spike** *is watching the pair of them. The things that can't be said pass between them . . . but only for a moment. She tilts her head and nods at him sadly, lightly smiles. And then the moment passes.* **Spike** *goes to* **Lizzie**.

Spike   What does it say, Lizzie?

Lizzie   How can a bird that is born for joy, sit in a cage and sing.

Spike   That's lovely. How . . . can . . . a . . . bird . . . that is born . . . for joy . . . sit . . . in . . . a cage . . . and sing!

Spike *points to the graffiti proudly.*

Spike   Look at me, I'm learning to read through vandalism!

As he seizes the microphone wildly to fill the empty air.

Out there in Liverpool there are a million broken windows and there are a million broken promises. They try and cast a spell like sleep-dust to make us all forget. They want to shatter our illusions, but we can break their spells by howling like wolves! If you want to come and join the party of dreamers and beggars, we are open. We are open! Come and join us if you dare . . .

Then he sprays the word 'OPN' above the broken Futurist neon, which is flickering as **Spike** *howls like a wolf.*

Scene Fourteen
METAFUCKINGMORPHOSIS

The present. One week later.

In the Futurist a strange and beautiful new vision is emerging from the ruins, but still the dust falls down. **Stephen** *and* **Lucas** *are moving a tattered silver screen into place. A banner hangs:* 'DISOBEDIENCE IS THE SPARK BEHIND ALL KNOWLEDGE'.

Lizzie   This is the Voice of Free Liverpool. Come and have your say. Broadcasting from the Futurist cinema. Just speak into the microphone . . . Everyone'll hear your voice, yes everyone, it's like being on Roger Phillips except no one interrupts . . .

City   I've got that crawling bugs feeling on my skin again. Five hundred thousand restless souls tormenting me and keeping me awake. Who am I talking to? I'll talk to you if you stand still long enough. About my aches and pains. About the bits of me ripped out by brutes and the parts of me left rotting . . . Who'd be a city in the north of England when the winter comes around . . . Five hundred years of insult and injury and no one ever listen . . . Centre of the consciousness of the universe? Thanks very much to the bastard who burdened me with that . . . You think it's easy being the city of Liverpool? It never stops raining, the wind's a curse, I stink of Subway salad dressing and I'm covered from head to toe in purple wheelie bins and pigeon shit. And nobody ever listens, do you . . . ?

She walks away, shaking her head in disappointment . . .

You'd listen to me if I was Barcelona . . .

As she switches off, **Spike** *turns up looking a bit battered and bruised.*

Spike   I got arrested. Again.

Stephen   What for this time?

Spike   For writing on walls.

Stephen   Vandalism?

Spike   Yeah . . . that's what the cop said. I said, 'Sorry about the poetry on walls.' But the cop just kept calling it vandalism. So I told him I can't really write. And I told him I can't read. And he said I could and I said I can't and he said . . .

Stephen   Yeah yeah, Spike . . .

Spike   He said, 'You appear to be writing poetry on derelict buildings,' and I said I was just copying words out of a book. This one . . .

He takes a book out of his pocket and gives it to **Stephen**.

Stephen   Ovid.

Spike   That's what the cop said. He said 'Ovid' just like
you did then. And I said I couldn't give a fuck, I was just
copying, brightening the city up a bit . . .

Lizzie   Enriching the city with poetry . . .

Spike   Exactly. And he said it was against the law. So I said,
writing beautiful poems on old buildings should be *compulsory*!
It should *be* the fucking law.

Stephen (*reads*)   'Of shapes transformed to bodies strange I
purpose to entreat . . . '

Spike   Exactly! Which is exactly what I meant when I told
the copper . . . So he said they'd catalogued at least fifty quotes
from poems on the walls of the city and I said, yes, they were
all done by me and he said why and I said: 'Human salvation
lies in the hands of the creatively maladjusted.' Martin Luther
King. I got that bit off Lizzie.

They stop and look at him and his constant gift for surprise.

Lizzie   And how did that go?

Spike   Well, it didn't go down that well, and then I said
'Fuck the Matrix' and then I was in the meat wagon and then
I was in the slammer and then I was up to me knees in shit if
I'm being honest, mate. So anyway, they asked for me address
and I said No Fixed Abode but then I said The Futurist
instead because I thought it sounded special like a toff and
they'd let me go. So then they're on to me and after information
but I kept me lip zipped . . .

Stephen   You were arrested for *transforming the city* . . .

Spike   I was arrested for magnificence.

Stephen   For *metafuckingmorphosis* . . .

Spike   I was arrested for *learning to write.*

Someone is knocking on the shutters. **Lizzie** *pulls up the shutter and* **Lucas** *dips in. In that moment the plaster crumbles worse than ever and dust falls down as* **Spike***'s graffiti slogans become visible.*

Dayglo graffiti slogans illuminate the Liverpool night.

But the building is giving up. **Lizzie** *watches the dust with sadness as it falls down in beams of light.* **Lucas** *goes up to* **Lizzie***.*

Lucas   Right. I'm just going to get on with it, Lizzie. I'm gonna say me piece and blaze in glory or say me piece and die in shame. Get it out in the open. Say your piece and blaze in glory or say your piece and die in shame . . . If I said you were the reason I came back, how would that go down?

Lizzie   Probably like a rock in a river . . . or a sack of cats in the canal.

Lucas   Perfect. Absolutely spot-on answer. Going well. Next question. If I said hardly a day goes by when I don't think about you, how would that go down?

Lizzie   Ha! Yeah, right. Every day?

Lucas   Sometimes . . .

Lizzie   Once a year? Now and then?

Lucas   Lots. Not in a weird way . . .

Lizzie   You could have come home any time. Could have come home to see your dad. Could have come to his funeral. What happened? Why now? Girlfriend dump you? Stop looking at me . . .

Lucas   I can remember your skin . . . like I said, not in a weird way.

Lizzie   You don't remember anything about me. I can tell.

Lucas   I can remember where your freckles are. Your constellation. Nine . . . no . . . ten freckles . . .

Lizzie   Oh piss off. Where?

Lucas   On your shoulder. There. Pretty as the stars.

This is almost a kind of held-breath flirtation. A feeling of danger. Beneath her words there is a sense that she is testing him despite the erotic tension. But she is not giving him anything.

Lizzie   I had them removed. Tattooed with bleach. They weren't a constellation, they were black hole stars.

Lucas   Show me your shoulder . . .

Lizzie   Get the fuck . . .

She adjusts her top, covering up. But he can see . . .

Lucas   They're still there.

Lizzie   Bloody useless tattoo parlour . . .

Lucas   I came back for you. Haven't exactly gone down a storm . . . but I'm telling the truth.

The temperature changes and whatever erotic tension there was between them is gone . . .

Lizzie   What, you suddenly learned to tell the truth? Long time ago we said we'd run away for ever. Kids say stupid things. Long time gone. Doesn't matter now . . . I've got me life. You don't know anything about me, Lucas. I've got a flat – in the Dingle. Oh yeah, and a paid-for fridge.

Lucas   You're right. I didn't know about your fridge . . .

Lizzie   You never asked. I don't sleep in the ruins like you bunch of deadbeats. I go home. I open me door – proper key, no crowbar – I *close* the door and think – this is mine! I open my fridge and I own that cheese. It's not much but it's mine. Flat, fridge, cheese. And I've got Calumn . . . I've got one wild kid in me life, why would I take on another?

Lucas   Ever been to Berlin? Fridges like Chevrolets. And the cheese! You'd love Berlin.

Lizzie   My Calumn wouldn't get in Berlin. They'd rebuild the wall to keep him out. And also, remembering my freckles? That's just sick. I wouldn't go to *Birkenhead* with a man who remembered freckles.

Lucas   OK. So, therefore this next bit's going too far. And I'm 'bout to make a show of meself. I've got something for you . . .

He takes a heart-shaped locket out of his pocket. She takes it, but just looks at it.

Lizzie   I don't want this. Is this a joke? Did you win this at the bingo?

Lucas   Wear it. Just try it on. All right, forget it, give it back. Give it to Elsie. Big mistake . . .

Lizzie   I just don't believe a word you say. Tell me something I'll believe . . .

Lucas   You've got flower seeds in your hair. Just like that night. Remember that? See, I remember that . . .

Lizzie   Ha, I remember too. Maybe they'll grow and I'll have a hair-do full of cornflowers, buttercups and daisies, hiding my grey hairs . . .

Lucas   You're beautiful already. I don't think I could cope if your hair was full of flowers . . .

Lizzie   Tell me something you *really* believe and then I'll tell you if I believe *you* . . .

Lucas   I lived the wrong life.

Lizzie   There's more life. Tomorrow. You could have that life if you fixed the past.

Lucas   That's what I want to do.

Lizzie   You should have fixed it years ago. You could have seen your dad and you could have gone and seen your mam. They kept asking for you but nobody knew where you were.

She starts to go. He calls after her.

Lucas   It was always you, Lizzie. I wanted to see you all the years I was away. So . . . I came home . . .

She turns to face him.

Lizzie   You ran away, Lucas. My brother died and you left us. No one knew where you'd gone. When someone dies like that their mates come together and, you know, grieve. But one of us was missing and we never, ever knew why. How do you think that feels? How do you think we felt – I felt – when you disappeared? Answer me. You can't, can you . . .

He reaches out to touch her . . .

Lucas   I see him . . .

Lizzie   What?

Lucas   Alan . . . His ghost . . .

She is shaken. She looks around the building where a skittering noise echoes in the shadows.

Lizzie   Don't do this to me . . .

This is the last straw . . .

Lucas   Lizzie, it's true . . .

But she's already walking away, here eyes pricking with tears. She reaches the cinema doorway.

Lizzie   No . . . Don't do this. I'm off to work, Lucas. You need to have a good think. But I'll tell you this. First chance you get, you'll run away. You don't know it yet, but you'll be gone for ever.

Lucas *goes to the door and watches her hurry away down the street.* **Elsie Barmaid** *has heard* **Lizzie**. *She watches her hurry away and then sees dejected* **Lucas** *going back inside.*

Elsie   Ah, now that's a sad, sad story that would be lovely in a song . . . the City's lullaby, Elsie singing it, sadly down back alleys in the heart of the night . . . And they don't know Elsie's watching and listening to their lives, and they don't know I've seen so many other lovers' broken hearts . . . Listen to me singing down the jigger, like a diva at the opera murmuring my song, like a bloody sad singer singing sad songs in the dark to broken loves . . .

And she lets a cloud of dust fall to earth.

Scene Fifteen
HEROIN

The past. 2 a.m.

Teenage years. **Alan** *is in an old chair in dimly lit shadows, lit by a glimmering candle in a bottle.* **Lucas** *comes in. There is aluminium foil, a lighter and a cigarette on an upturned crate.*

Alan   Been anywhere nice?

Lucas   Down the cut. Buying a bag.

Alan   Seen anything of our Lizzie? Me dad's going mad. Cos she should be home doing the tea.

Lucas   She'll be home in time to spit in his Guinness . . .

Alan   Like our mam used to do before she left us like dogs.

Lucas *sits down. They smoke and slug beer from cans.* **Lucas** *takes out a bag of powder, shakes it and looks at the paraphernalia.*

Lucas   You sure about this?

Alan   It's your call, mate. I'm up for anything.

They look at each other.

Lucas   Fuck it . . .

Alan   Yeah. Fuck it.

Alan   What does it feel like?

Lucas   They say it's like forbidden fruit. Ten minutes from now you'll be flying.

He stubs out his cigarette and takes the foil and tube. He just sits there drinking from his can. He doesn't smoke.

Scene Sixteen
PARTY TIME

The present. Saturday. Bonfire night, 10 p.m.

Lucas *is pulling barricades of corrugated metal into place.* **Calumn** *is spinning wheelies on his stunt bike. Inside the musicians are soundchecking.* **Lucas** *calls to* **Calumn**.

Lucas   Hey, kid! Calumn!

Calumn   Whatever, old arse!

Lucas   What happened to me jacket?

Calumn   Not wearing that old thing. Smells like road-kill. Sold it to a mug.

He gives **Lucas** *the finger and speeds away. Flashing lights bounce off the walls of Lime Street. Trouble is coming.*

Inside the Futurist **Stephen** *is setting up a rough stage out of crates and scrap.* **Spike** *is dragging scrap and salvage from derelict buildings into the space.* **Lizzie** *has headphones on, listening to a broadcast. She takes the cans off and turns to the others.*

Lizzie   Just picking up on police radio. Apparently we're an illegal gathering!

Spike   Aw, I love it!

Stephen   This is gonna be like a mad cabaret at midnight. It's gonna be like Ziggy Stardust raided by the filth! It's gonna be like a building on drugs!

Spike   We'll open the building to everyone . . .

Stephen   Drag queens! Midnight howlers!

Spike   And all them dogs and madmen that fell through the crack in the ground . . .

He's wearing **Lucas**'s *leather jacket, collar up. He empties his pockets. The casements of fireworks spill on to the ground.*

Spike (*sings*)   Light up the sky with Standard Fireworks!

He takes out a packet of sparklers, passes them out and lights them. They all stand in the dark with their sparklers lighting up the place, waving them around.

Spike I love sparklers! . . . I feel a bit sad.

They look at him. He's emotional.

Bit sad, yeah. But it's all right crying. It's all right getting a bit upset.

Sometimes at night I used to climb into bed and be on me own and feel sad things about meself. But you know, now it's all right because we've got all this and we're doing this thing. And I've got me reading and writing now. And it feels a bit important. Doing this thing. And here we are. Together . . .

And now I kind of am happy. Happy in a way that's also sad . . .

And the thing is, it's all right being me.

Being Spike.

They all look at him as if it's the most profound thing they've ever heard – and in a way, it is. **Lizzie** *is shivering. She looks around as if for* **Alan**'s *ghost.* **Spike** *takes off* **Lucas**'s *leather jacket and drapes it over her shoulders tenderly.* **Lucas** *comes in like the wind.* **Spike** *calls to him.*

Spike Look at me new jacket Luke! Bought it off Lizzie's lad. £29.99. How cool am I gonna look next time I'm on the telly?!

Lucas What the fuck's going on, Spike? There are men in high-viz jackets everywhere. Cops parked up outside the comic shop. This your doing?

Spike I just told them me address again. Not the psychiatric unit cos I'm barred. This place.

Lucas Oh well done, Spike . . .

Spike Yeah, I thought you'd be pleased.

Stephen   Don't get on Spike's case, Lucas! You're the
pirate radio man telling everyone we're here . . .

Spike   Oh I see, you saying I'd betray you, Luke? You
saying you don't trust me? We have to trust each other, mate.
I trusted you with my glass eye in case you've forgotten . . .

Lizzie   Bloody hell, Lucas! Spike's the last man who'd
betray us. He just gets a bit over-excitable.

Spike   I'm sociable in an anti-social way.

Lizzie   We're all in this together and no one here would
ever let us down.

Spike   Hey! Look, no harm done . . . Come on. It's
bommie night.

Stephen   Harm done to you. Every time you turn up
you've got another bit missing.

Lucas   There'll be harm done if those bastards come
after us . . .

Lizzie   We'll harm them before they mess with us.

Spike *drapes fairy lights around his shoulders.*

Spike   They'll wet themselves when they see they're dealing
with a one-eyed nutter fairy-light display and a cabaret singer
in a dress!

They look to **Lucas**.

Lizzie   And where will you be, Lucas?

Spike   He'll be here. Leave it. We'll all be here. Us and the
dogs and howling men, pouring out from the bowels of the
earth. Right. Enough.

*He lights the sparkler with a match and it's beautiful in the dark. He
quietly enjoys his sparkler. He sits there smiling, draped in fairy lights,
which flicker on and illuminate the dust that falls from the rafters as the
building sighs and dies a little more . . .* **Lucas** *goes to* **Spike**.

Lucas   We're done for, Spike. Look at the place. It's falling to pieces. We're kidding ourselves.

Stephen   We can't give up . . .

Spike   Yeah, what about your squatting days in Amsterdam? You were a hero!

Lucas   But they were different times . . .

They look at him. A bit disappointed.

Stephen   Why were they different, Lucas?

Lucas   When you're younger, you're wilder . . .

Spike *actually looks hurt. Let down . . .*

Spike   Since when did you stop being wild? We have to stick this out as long as we can. You can't leave old ladies to die alone. This is the best thing we've ever done since we were kids.

Lucas   We're still acting like kids. I mean, look at us . . . freezing to death in a dying cinema. We're hungry and filthy. We never sleep. No one gives a fuck what we do.

Spike   Oh, they do, you know. I was out buying a can of meat to feed the dogs down the drain . . .

Stephen   There are no dogs down the drain!

Spike   Yes, there are. I'm gonna give them names. Anyway, some fella in a suit give me this. (*Takes out a letter.*) I said I can't read properly. He said, give it to a responsible adult.

He gives it to **Lizzie**, *who reads it. She passes it to* **Lucas**.

Lizzie   It's a warning to vacate the premises.

Spike   I've got that it's-all-gonna-kick-off feeling. I love that feeling!

Lizzie   I don't want to lose this fight.

Lucas   We have lost it, Liz. You can't bring dead things back to life.

Spike   You used to. If you're not going to, we will . . .

Calumn *rides up on his stunt bike, a bow and arrow strapped to his back.*

Calumn   You'll know they're coming. They'll cordon off the streets. Make it look like road works. What you need to do is get in first. I can get you a couple of buckets of butyric acid . . .

Nasty business.

Lucas   What you're saying is . . .

Calumn (*shrugs*)   It's just an option. Use the weapon on the aggressor before they use it on you. Get yourself some bombs.

He looks at their ancient faces . . .

Lucas   You take after your mother . . .

Calumn   Get organised, you old get! Get your Twitter account going. Set up your Facebook page . . .

Spike   Can you get your hands on a water cannon?

Calumn   I'll put the word out.

He gets his phone out and starts texting until **Lizzie** *holds her hand out and he surrenders the phone. She holds her hand out again . . .*

Lizzie   And your pay-as-you-go . . . and your bow and arrow . . .

He surrenders his spare phone and then reluctantly his weapons. **Stephen** *is draping himself in exotic costume and head-dress.*

Stephen   They wouldn't come for us . . . would they?

Lucas   Course they will. They'll smoke us out like cockroaches . . .

Spike   OK, so that's a bucket-of-vomit bomb, a water cannon . . .

Stephen *straps on a home-made tear-gas mask fashioned from a plastic bottle.*

Stephen   I'm thinking tear-gas mask made from plastic bottle mixed with tribal head-dress. I'm thinking masks and metal wings like Alan had and singing anarcho-karaoke through fuck-off megaphones. I'm thinking nothing fancy . . .

But he's got nothing on **Elsie**, *who is arriving like a goddess.*

Stephen   Oh sweet heaven, will you look at this!

Elsie Barmaid *comes in, looking beautiful. They look at her in awe.*

Stephen   If the Aztecs had cabaret singers . . .

Lizzie   We might be beaten but at least we've got Elsie. (*To* **Lucas**.) So, we carry on, yes?

Lucas   Yeah . . . OK. Let's do it. Let's fill the city streets with Elsie's song.

Spike   Victory to the Awkward Bastards!

Lucas (*uncertain*)   Victory to the Awkward Bastards, yeah . . .

Stephen *steps forward and drapes* **Elsie** *in a glittering gown.*

Elsie   I'm looking for Glenn Ford.

Lucas   Hello Elsie . . . you look beautiful.

Elsie   I'm ready for my song.

Lucas *nods and takes her to the microphone stand. She pushes her trolley. Then she unpacks a few things. She takes out her mirror and looks at herself.*

Elsie   I'm beautiful again. Like the girl I used to be.

Lucas *nods, smiles.* **Elsie** *looks around and sighs.*

Elsie   In the spring it will be lovely here, when the wild flowers grow.

She waves at the ruins.

Stephen   What would you like to perform for us this evening?

Elsie   I want to sing like Rita Hayworth.

Stephen *nods, bows to her and speaks into the microphone.*

Stephen   Ladies and gentlemen! Welcome to Bright
Phoenix! Broadcasting live from the resurrected Futurist
Cinema . . . For your delight and delectation on this wonderful
evening . . . I give you the Siren of Lime Street, the Torch
Singer of the Midnight City, the Divine Goddess of Song . . .
Miss Elsie!

Applause. The music starts to play. The party is kicking off. **Elsie** *sings
in spotlight, beneath a mirror ball. As she sings* **Lucas** *takes his old
leather jacket off a heap and puts it on. He quietly picks up his rucksack
and takes one last look round. And then he slips away, unnoticed by the
others, apart from* **Spike** *who picks up the crystal radio and goes after him.*

Elsie
>   When they had the earthquake in San Francisco
>   Back in nineteen-six
>   They said that Mother Nature
>   Was up to her old tricks
>   That's the story that went around
>   But here's the real low down
>
>   Put the blame on Mame, boys
>   Put the blame on Mame
>   One night she started to shim and shake
>   That brought on the Frisco quake
>   So you can put the blame on Mame, boys
>
>   Put the blame on Mame

It's heart-breakingly beautiful as **Elsie** *dances and sings. She gets to the
end of her song and* **Pete the Piss** *sways forth and presents her with a
bouquet of buddleia and willow herb. She bows like a diva. He blows her
a kiss and swaggers away.* **Stephen** *goes to* **Elsie**.

Stephen   That was beautiful . . . so beautiful.

Elsie   I've never been so happy and I've never been so
proud . . .

Stephen   What are you going to do?

Elsie   This evening? Or with the rest of my life?

Stephen   Both.

Elsie   First I'm going to leave the bus shelter. And then I'm going to walk among the stars.

She bows with her bouquet. There is the sound of a police helicopter overhead, drowning out the music and blowing dust and debris everywhere.

Lucas *is at the entrance when* **Spike** *notices, goes after him, carrying his crowbar and the crystal radio.* **Lizzie** *watches* **Lucas** *going,* **Spike** *going after him. She starts to go after them, tentatively, but then she feels the air change. She looks around.* **Alan** *is there, watching over her. She can't see him but she can feel him.*

Spike *catches up with* **Lucas** *and does a double-take when he sees* **Lucas** *is wearing the leather jacket. He's emotional.*

Spike   Lucas! So you're going then?

He holds up his crowbar.

Spike   Do you want me spare key, in case you come back?

Lucas *(smiles sadly)*   Bit like the end of *Shane* this . . . 'Come back, Shane, come back . . . '

Spike   So come back, Lucas . . . what'll we do without you?

Lucas   You did without me for twenty years . . .

Spike   You'll be needing your crystal radio.

He holds the radio.

Lucas   Keep it. Look after it till next time.

Spike   Is it cos I snore? Is that it?

Lucas *takes* **Spike** *and pulls him close into his arms. A moment. And then . . .*

Lucas   Look after each other, Spike. Until the next time comes around.

Spike *watches him go and gives a sad, faltering wave goodbye.*

Spike   Don't step on the cracks!

He wipes his eyes on his sleeve.

Fucker's still got me glass eye.

The fairy light stars shine down.

Scene Seventeen
THE FLIGHT OF ICARUS

Midnight. The past and present collide.

Lucas *is walking down the night street, searching the gutters for discarded fags, when he encounters* **Alan**, *dressed in all his winged beauty. They eye each other warily,* **Lucas** *weighing things up carefully.*

Alan   Guess what I did Lucas? Guess what I did when I was sick of being me? I took a hypodermic needle and I sucked the blood out of a dead gull. A syringe full of bird blood. And then I found a vein . . .

He flexes his fingers and taps a vein. He mimes a hypodermic in his other hand and jacks up.

And I pumped the bird's blood into my system. Felt it rush through my veins like wild glory hurtling through my body. I got jacked up on bird blood. Wilder than whisky, wilder than high-grade heroin. I turn into a bird. Imagine that!

I am flying. I swoop over the rooftops of Liverpool, over the waterfront and out to sea, following a trawler as it drags its nets through the wild sea. I am a seventeen-year-old bird boy, addicted to seagull blood, flying through sea-storms, up to the moon.

He is shimmering, beautiful.

> Dark wings, falling hawk
> Pulling the sky down
> Faster than weapon.

I am the hawk boy.
My name is Icarus.

My name is Alan Icarus!
And I can fucking fly!

He steps into the void . . .

Lucas   No!

Lucas's *voice echoes as he reaches up towards* **Alan**, *who is walking into space. He seems to hover there for a moment, in the air, beating his wild wings . . .*

Lucas *moves towards him as if to try and catch him . . .*

Lucas
And he's laughing as he flies. As he falls.
And I run. I run as far as I can go.
And I dream about him falling.
Always falling.
For ever.

He turns and runs away as **Alan** *flies . . . and falls as if for ever.*

Silence.

Scene Eighteen
THE FINAL BROADCAST

The present. Later that night, the party still in flow.

A woman is singing softly, somewhere in the shadows. Outside the cinema a sign covers the entrance: DEMOLITION SITE — DO NOT ENTER.

Inside the Futurist **Spike** *gets on his soapbox and speaks into the microphone. A Lime Street man –* **Jimmy** *– turns up and watches, listens as* **Spike** *speaks to the people of Liverpool, to the people gathered in the cinema, to us.*

Jimmy *gets on the microphone.*

Jimmy   I used to be the projectionist in this cinema and here I spent my life. It was here I met my lovely wife, we courted here when we were young and old . . . But what happened to her was she faded away and nobody nursed her but me . . . and every time I walk past this building I think of her and how I tried to keep her alive with love . . . Like this fella said, what this place means is people, and, guess what, we are the people and we own this city. In our hearts and imaginations we own this city's bones. And that's what's missing from their souls. Imagination. They've got no imagination. Crying, crying, crying, crying shame.

Spike   And it hurts doesn't it?

Jimmy   Damn right it hurts!

It makes you feel sad inside because it matters, this place where people join together. Isn't that right, mate?

Jimmy   Yeah, it is. It's a crying fucking shame.

Spike   But even as it dies it's beautiful, this building. And the idea that people need to get together in the pictures, in the pub, in the street, is a beautiful idea.

Jimmy   Yes! It's a beauty. An absolute beauty.

Spike   This has been the Voice of Free Liverpool. It's been a hell of a night . . . Over and out.

He switches off. He turns to the old man.

Jimmy   Have you got a new name for the old place mate?

Spike   Yeah. It's called Bright Phoenix.

He takes off his shirt and written on his chest is:

DO NOT BETRAY YOUR DREAMS

He stands back and admires his handiwork.

Spike   Leonardo Da fucking Vinci.

Then **Spike** *and* **Jimmy** *the projectionist turn and give high-fives. The musicians strike up. A beautiful song and perhaps a time for dancing . . .*

Scene Nineteen
BRIGHT PHOENIX

The present.

Inside the Futurist they move through the rubble and dust. The musicians are still playing. It's like a party in the ruins of civilisation.

Spike   It's either over or it's the beginning. It's time . . .

Stephen *and* **Lizzie** *appear dressed in incredible capes and gowns, shamanistic head-dresses and tear-gas masks. They look like miraculous gods. They have a costume for* **Spike** *too and they place a corrugated sheet on his back like a metal warrior's cape.*

One by one the gang become visible in the cinema ruins as the dust billows around them. They walk through the rubble and dust. **Spike** *gazes up through the broken rooftop at the sky above.*

Spike   I'm looking at things but I don't know what they're called.

Stephen   They're called *stars*, Spike. As in twinkle twinkle.

Spike   I know they're stars but I don't know their names. Name the stars, Ste. If you want to . . . if you want to . . .

Stephen   Tonight the stars are awkward bastards . . . (*Gently.*) That bright one twinkling over the lap-dancing club?

He points out the stars . . .

That one's Rosa Luxemburg . . .

Spike   She's a new one!

Stephen   Next to her is Emmeline Pankhurst . . . Boudicca . . . Asmaa Mahfouz . . .

Spike   Name one after me, Ste!

Stephen   You're not a woman, you bucket! That one's Joan of Arc . . . next to her is Rosa Parks . . . I'm gonna call that one Elsie . . .

Spike   What about our Lizzie?

Lizzie   You can't name a star after me . . .

Stephen   Who says we can't? We can do anything we want.

Softly singing and pointing at the star.

Lizzie Flynn . . .

Oh Lizzie bloody Flynn . . .

It's beautiful. They wish upon the stars. **Stephen** *is crying softly . . .*

Spike   What's the do, Ste? Is it the beauty?

Stephen   Yeah, it's the beauty . . .

Spike   Come here, Ste, and I'll wrap you in me arms . . .

He hands **Stephen** *a filthy handkerchief.* **Stephen** *blows his nose. Then* **Spike** *wraps him in his arms for a moment until a great rumbling comes from outside, the sound of a police helicopter and then a deafening banging on steel shutters.*

Stephen   It's the orchestra of hell . . .

Spike   It's that rent-asunder moment when the earth opens up and the wild beasts come spewing out . . .

Lizzie   It's the police.

They stand up. They take up pots and pans, scrap metal, hubcaps, car parts. And then they beat. Echoing. ECHOING. **Spike** *beats with his crowbar. They beat on the barricades with hammers, beat on* **Spike**'s *cape of corrugated metal. Louder and louder, an ecstatic, ritualistic, infernal racket, amplified, reverberating. They move forward through the space and then they stand their ground. The beating of metal gets louder, louder, ecstatic and echoing. Loud as metal thunder as smoke fills the air. They sing . . .*

THE CHOIR OF THE CHIMNEYS

Down chimney twenty-nine
A child is wept to sleep
The vouchers come on Wednesday
And then the mother eats

Down chimney forty-two
The advert break is loud
Loan sharks in the telly
And their meat is on the couch

Listen to the choir of the chimneys fill the room

Down chimney eighty-eight
A nest of twig and bone
The chicks have fledged, the parents gone
Another empty home

Listen to the choir of the chimneys fill the sky

Down chimney twenty-five
The walls are lies themselves
One room split into four
People sleeping on the shelves

Listen to the choir of the chimneys fill your bones

The clouds are filling with these stories full of rage
The rumble's building, but it's not water that will rain
They'll rag their voices till their throats are bursted through
Leave others to lie
They only sing of what's true
Leave others to lie
They only sing of what's true

A whirling murmuration of starlings swoops and dances over their heads. And then the sound of howling dogs. **Spike** *is in ecstatic mode as the ground tears itself up and the volatile scar in the ground spews open.*

Spike   O earthly powers that pierce men to their hearts, let wild beasts and birds spill out and roam this city!

After a while the noises cease and an echoing silence takes their place as dawn breaks and the new sun spills its beams into the ruins. **Lizzie**, **Stephen** *and* **Spike** *look at the beautiful ruins of their Bright Phoenix. They stand amidst rubble, scrap metal, boxes and broken things – the debris salvaged from old buildings, stacked in the shape of a scrapheap aeroplane in the billowing smoke and flickering flames.* **Lizzie** *picks up a handful of dirt and lets it fall.*

Lizzie   Beneath the paving stones the beach . . .

Stephen   Sous les paves, la plage!

Spike *guides* **Lizzie** *to a heap of rubble. She stands on it as if it were a soapbox. The Futurist is in ruins. She begins to speak, tentatively, sadly.*

Lizzie
    We built this Bright Phoenix out of dead cinemas . . .
    Out of derelict pub saloons and the burned-out shells of
        churches . . .
    Out of the ghost ruins of this magnificent city . . .
    Out of abandoned libraries . . .

She grows increasingly dignified and proud . . .

    Out of the ballrooms of desire and the music halls and
        cabarets . . .
    Out of the floorboards and pews of old theatres . . .
    Out of the ruins of the houses we were born in . . .
    Out of the abandoned glories of this city . . .
    Out of our despair at the deathly lack of dreamers . . .
    Out of our desire to ignite imaginations . . .
    Out of our great and glorious endeavours and our desire
        to do something astonishing . . .

All
    Great and glorious endeavours and our desire to do
        something astonishing!

They stand there in the ruins. Their voices echo. The crack in Lime Street is alive with light and shadows. Music pours through the fallen building.

As if in celebration of the youthful wildness that still burns in their hearts **Lizzie** *and* **Stephen** *climb into the aeroplane – just like they did when they were kids.* **Spike** *picks up the crystal radio set and climbs in too. He puts the headphones on.*

Stephen   Permission to take off, Group Captain?

Spike   It's a wild and stormy day here in Liverpool and the dust is rising high but we'll risk it! Ten Four. Over.

Stephen   Bumpy start . . . taxi-ing down the runway, the battered old bomber plane shaking . . . lifting from the ground . . .

Lizzie   Lick the battery! Over . . .

She takes a battery from her pocket, passes it round and they all lick it.

They rattle and shake. **Spike** *presses controls. They fly through old films.* **Calumn** *rides through the building on his stunt bike.* **Elsie** *watches them go . . .*

Stephen   And in our dreams we are airborne, slipping the bonds of the earth, a phoenix rising from the ashes, flying on a wing and a prayer over the rooftops of Liverpool, embracing the elemental eternity of heaven . . .

ROGER. TEN FOUR. OVER AND OUT!

They fly in their wild imaginations as if over the city.

And the Futurist sign flickers and glows.

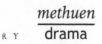

For a complete listing of Bloomsbury
Methuen Drama titles, visit:
www.bloomsbury.com/drama

Follow us on Twitter and keep up to date
with our news and publications
@MethuenDrama